Also by Twyla Tharp

The Creative Habit: Learn It and Use It for Life

Push Comes to Shove: An Autobiography

THE COLLABORATIVE HABIT

Life Lessons for Working Together

TWYLA THARP

with Jesse Kornbluth

Simon & Schuster

New York   London   Toronto   Sydney

Simon & Schuster
1230 Avenue of the Americas
New York, NY 10020

First Simon & Schuster hardcover edition November 2009

SIMON & SCHUSTER and colophon are registered trademarks of Simon & Schuster, Inc.

Credits for photographs: Page 2, photograph © Martha Swope; pages 18–19, courtesy of the author; page 34, *White Nights* © 1985 Columbia Pictures Industries, Inc. All rights reserved. Courtesy of Columbia Pictures; page 46, photograph by Manny Hernandez; pages 74–75, photograph by Gene Schiavone; pages 92–93, photograph by Marc von Borstel; pages 112–13, photograph by Michael Weller.

For information about special discounts for bulk purchases, please contact Simon & Schuster Special Sales at 1-866-506-1949 or business@simonandschuster.com.

The Simon & Schuster Speakers Bureau can bring authors to your live event. For more information or to book an event, contact the Simon & Schuster Speakers Bureau at 1-866-248-3049 or visit our website at www.simonspeakers.com.

Designed by Julian Peploe Studio

Manufactured in the United States of America

10 9 8 7 6 5 4 3 2 1

Library of Congress Cataloging-in-Publication Data
Tharp, Twyla.
The Collaborative Habit / Twyla Tharp.
p. cm.
1. Partnership. 2. Cooperativeness. 3. Teams in the workplace.
4. Artistic collaboration. 5. Tharp, Twyla. I. Title.
HD69.S8T45 2009
650.1'3—dc2   2009033501

ISBN 978-1-4165-7650-1
ISBN 978-1-4165-9191-7 (ebook)

To my son, Jesse Alexander Huot. A collaboration better by the day.

Two are better than one; because they have a good reward for their labor.

—Ecclesiastes 4:9

CONTENTS

THE COLLABORATIVE HABIT

CHAPTER 1

What It Is, Why It Matters, Why It's the Future

I'm a choreographer who makes dances that are performed on stages around the world. It's just as accurate to say I'm a career collaborator. That is, I identify problems, organize them, and solve them by working with others. Many of the stories I'll be telling involve the world of dance, but you don't have to know anything about dance to get the point. Work is work.

I define collaboration as people working together—sometimes by choice, sometimes not. Sometimes we collaborate to jump-start creativity; other times the focus is simply on getting things done. In each case, people in a good collaboration accomplish more than the group's most talented members could achieve on their own.

Here's a classic example of someone who identified a problem and worked with others to solve it. The year was 1962. The problem was a new play, *A Funny Thing Happened on the Way to the Forum*. The collaborator was Jerome Robbins, the choreographer and director who later became my good friend and coworker.

As *A Funny Thing* was completing its pre-Broadway tour, no one was laughing. Not Stephen Sondheim, who wrote the music and lyrics. Not veteran director George Abbott. Certainly not producer Hal Prince and the play's backers.

And, most important of all, not the audience.

At the Washington previews, just three weeks before the New York opening, audiences were fleeing the theater. By the time the curtain came down, the theater was often only half full.

And yet, on paper, *A Funny Thing* should have been a huge hit—the creative team couldn't have been more distinguished.

What was wrong? No one knew.

What to do? That they knew.

When a show has script trouble, it's common for the producers to bring in a "play doctor." In business, he'd be called a consultant. I'd call him a collaborator—someone who works with others to solve a problem.

The doctor they called in was Jerome Robbins, who came to Washington from Los Angeles, where he had just collected an Academy Award for *West Side Story*. He watched a performance—and by intermission, not only had he analyzed the problem, he had a solution.

A Funny Thing, Robbins said, was a farce inspired by the comedies of Plautus, a Roman playwright. But Plautus lived from 254 to 184 . . . before Christ. How many theatergoers knew who he was? Or what kind of plays he wrote? And, most of all, who knew what kind of play *A Funny Thing Happened on the Way to the Forum* was supposed to be?

Jerome Robbins offered simple, commonsense advice: *It's a comedy. Tell them that.*

Sondheim quickly wrote an opening number called "Comedy Tonight"—"Something convulsive / Something repulsive / Something for everyone: a comedy tonight!"—and once ticket buyers knew what they were supposed to do, they laughed. The New York reviews were cheers for an "uninhibited romp," and *A Funny Thing* played 964 performances on Broadway before going off to Hollywood and becoming a hit movie.

Clearly, it's a good idea to tell people what to expect.

Here's what you can expect from this book: a field guide to a lot of the issues that surface when you are working in a collaborative environment. I'll

5

explain why collaboration is important to me—and, I'll bet, to you. I'll show you how to recognize good candidates to work with and how you build a successful collaboration—and I'll share what it feels like to be trapped in a dysfunctional one. And, finally, although this isn't a book that promises to help you find love or deepen your romantic life, I suspect that some of what you may learn from these pages can help you in your personal relationships. In each case, because collaboration isn't an airy concept but a practice that's found in our daily reality, I'll be light on ideas and heavy on stories.

> Collaboration is how most of our ancestors used to work and live, before machines came along and fragmented society.

Time to plant the fields? Everybody pitched in and got it done. Harvesttime? The community raced to get the crops in before the rains came. Where were those crops stored? In barns built by teams of neighbors.

In the cities, the same spirit applied. Anonymous craftsmen spent their lives building cathedrals that wouldn't be completed for generations. Michelangelo is celebrated for the Sistine Chapel; in fact, he supervised a dozen unacknowledged assistants. Even one of the greatest composers, Johann Sebastian Bach, chose to deflect credit for his compositions, writing at the bottom of each of his pieces "SDG," for *Soli Deo Gloria*—to God alone the glory.

By the twentieth century, only a few self-isolated sects practiced the collaborative tradition. Blame it on wars that killed millions, the atomic bomb, Freud, or any combination of factors you choose—there's no shortage of reasons. The result is that most of us grew up in a culture that applauded only individual achievement. We are, each of us, generals in an ego-driven "army of one," each the center of an absurd cosmos, taking such happiness as we can find. Collaboration? Why bother? You only live once; grab whatever you can.

But now more and more of us are realizing that the brilliant CEO, the politician who keeps his own counsel, and the lone hero are yesterday's role models. The media may still love them, but our new heroes are men and women who know how to gather allies, build teams, and work together toward shared goals. Name an enterprise, and you'll find levels of collaboration that were unthinkable just a few years ago. The real success stories of our time are about joint efforts: sports teams, political campaigns, businesses, causes.

Collaboration is the buzzword of the new millennium.

Like many of you, I went to school when victory meant raising your hand first and shouting out the answer—school was a war zone that rewarded only the brightest and most aggressive. But now learning is collaborative; children work together in groups to solve problems. They solve them faster this way, and without winners or losers. And in doing so, they gain valuable life skills.

Consider the Internet, which has dramatically increased our ability to communicate with friends and associates—and millions of strangers around the world. Now we can form networks and create collaborations without start-up money, an infrastructure, or even an office. Result? Our basic urge to work in groups can be realized more easily now than at any time in modern history.

Thanks to the Internet, a battered economy, and a profound shift in personal values, a notion that was once heresy—that the wisdom of a smart group is greater than the brainpower of its smartest member—is increasingly accepted in every discipline and every profession and at every age and stage of life.

On the Internet, someone posts an article, then others comment. With the addition of new facts and points of view, readers benefit—and by contributing to the conversation, they become part of a smart community.

In business, "crowdsourcing"—assigning a task that used to be done by a single worker to whole communities—has become a powerful tool in the product-development process.

Dell Computers, for example, created an outreach called IdeaStorm to get ideas and feedback from customers. So far, the company has used almost three hundred of their suggestions—keyboards that light up in the dark, more color choices, longer battery life—in its new products.

Starbucks has launched a Web site called My Starbucks Idea to gather consumer brainstorms, filter them through management, and then have the coffee company's customers vote on the best ones. The site has collected seventy thousand suggestions.

In politics, the 2008 presidential campaign of Barack Obama proved that the most powerful word in his slogan, "Yes we can," was *we*.

Until 2008, most politicians used the Internet only for fund-raising. Barack Obama, a former community organizer, saw that "social networking" could mean more than the exchange of trivial blasts of personal information by virtual "friends." And he used the Web to build a movement that transformed interest into participation.

Obama's site had double the traffic of opponent John McCain's. Four times as many visitors to YouTube watched Obama's videos. He had five times as many Facebook "friends." Three million people signed up for his text messages—and he sent them fifteen to twenty a month. And in the last four days of the campaign, Obama campaign volunteers made three million personal phone calls.

Experts say that no political campaign, no matter how well funded, could generate that much content on its own. Obama's core Internet team consisted of just eleven people. The rest of the work was done by highly committed supporters who took the communication devices they used every day and repurposed them to rally their personal networks for a common cause.

In sports it has always been about the team.

Michael Jordan started winning scoring titles in 1986. But the Chicago Bulls were not winning championships. Bulls Coach Phil Jackson knew why: "Scoring champions don't win championships." The team brought in some stronger players. And although Michael Jordan was already recognized as the greatest player in the history of basketball, he started moving the ball around. In 1991, the Bulls won their first championship in franchise history. That year, Jordan was voted the most valuable player in the finals in part because he scored thirty points in the deciding game—but also because, in the same game, he passed the ball to teammates for ten assists.

You are probably not a professional basketball player or a politician or the proprietor of an Internet news site. You probably don't run a high-tech company or make educational policy for a school district. But in the last few years, you've certainly been exposed to the notion that collaboration is all-pervasive and you're wondering how it applies to you—especially if you have not picked the people you work with and report to a remote, unhelpful boss.

So your first question may be as simple as this: I'm trapped in a job that has me assigned to a team made up of impossible people. I need the salary and the benefits. How can I get along with these colleagues so I deliver good work and advance?

The answer is that it's no different for you than it is for the players on a championship sports team or a crew of genius scientists or, for that matter, dancers in leotards rehearsing a new ballet.

People are people. And people are problems. But—and this is a very big but—people who are practiced in collaboration will do better than those who insist on their individuality.

Consider, for example, the "hero" of that miraculous emergency landing of a passenger jet in New York's Hudson River.

After geese damaged the engines of his plane shortly after takeoff, US Airways' Captain Chesley Sullenberger managed to guide the jet with its 155 passengers and crew to a safe landing on the water.

A few months later, at an aviation safety hearing to learn why no one died, the captain was asked, "This event turned out differently than a lot of the situations the board has looked at. What made the critical difference in this event? How did this event turn out so well?"

Captain Sullenberger's response: "I don't think it was one thing; it was many things. We had a highly experienced, well-trained crew. The first officer, Jeffrey Skiles, and I worked together well as a team and we solved each problem as it presented itself to us."

Look at the key words in that response: *experience . . . crew . . . team*. Sullenberger couldn't be clearer. He might be a media darling and a national hero, but he viewed this successful landing as the collaborative triumph of a practiced group.

But note: You can't force people to collaborate. You can make them share offices and serve on committees together, but if their hearts aren't in it, the process is an empty shell. Personal, emotional commitment is crucial.

Collaborators aren't born, they're made. Or, to be more precise, built, a day at a time, through practice, through attention, through discipline, through passion and commitment—and, most of all, through habit.

A book I wrote a few years ago, *The Creative Habit*, began with an account of what was then my daily ritual. Up at 5:50 A.M. A cab ride to a gym across town. And then two hours of stretching and weight training. After that, I was ready to be a choreographer.

This account of my daily routine shocked some readers. People want to believe that the creative habit has something to do with creating—making dance, writing music or fiction, painting a great picture, forming a successful business. Instead, I was pointing to everything that came before the dance, before the writing, before the painting: preparedness, getting ready for the job of creating—because creating isn't some exalted process, it's a grimy job. Manual labor. Heavy lifting. And as those who do physical work know, the more routine it feels, the better.

That's an extremely unromantic view of creativity. When my friend and collaborator Milos Forman filmed *Amadeus,* he showed you Mozart as a prodigy, maybe the greatest ever. He didn't show you how Mozart became Mozart—you wouldn't have liked that story. Because the truth is, Mozart wasn't born a "genius." His father recognized that the boy had talent, and he pushed him—hard. By the time Mozart was twenty-eight years old, his hands were deformed because of all the hours he had spent practicing, performing, and gripping a quill pen to compose.

Like creativity, collaboration is a habit—and one I encourage you to develop. At first it may seem unnatural to show up and care more about a collaborative project than about your personal advancement, but once you start ignoring your comfort level, you're on your way. Even if your collaborators are smarter than you? More hardworking? Quicker-thinking? More imaginative? Yes. It's like playing tennis; you improve only when you play above your level.

So if you have any say in the matter, gravitate to people who are smart and caring. Watch them, learn from them. And see if you don't soon feel that, far from being burdened with a partner, you're beginning to find new options and new ways of thinking.

Thinking? Collaboration may be a practice—a way of working in harmony with others—but it begins as a point of view. Could your relationships be better? Consider this first: You might be the problem (or a big part of it).

The Buddhist philosopher Thich Nhat Hanh deals bluntly with the first reason you might be having trouble: You put yourself first—but you don't love yourself enough. He quotes the Buddha: "The moment you see how important it is to love yourself, you will stop making others suffer."

How do you love yourself more?

Thich Nhat Hanh says, "Stop treating yourself like an enemy." Well, consider your self-esteem. Skip your problems—we all have them—and examine only your general feelings about yourself. Do you have generous, compassionate feelings toward your friends, relatives, and romantic partners? Can you share with them in ways that give you tools to work with others? Are you so "honest" that you alienate people? In a group, do you share information? Confront problems openly? Support the mission?

It's easy enough to claim that we all want to be part of something bigger than ourselves, that we want to do well and do good. But as much as we are all similar, we're also unique. Do you have the temperament to be on a team? Or do others exist simply to get you the ball so you're the one who shoots and scores?

If you don't like other people and don't trust group activity, you're going to have a problem in a collaborative environment. Change your attitude and see if others don't respond.

Over four decades, I have worked with thousands of dancers and almost a hundred companies—in 2008, the especially intense year that I'll be talking about frequently in these pages, I made four new works for three different companies to the music of four composers, two of these newly commissioned scores. I've experienced the thrill of shared achievement and seen what happens when group efforts fizzle. My professional life has been—and continues to be—one collaboration after another.

I work with lawyers, designers, composers, sponsoring ballet companies, the directors of those ballet companies, and, not least, the audience. When the curtain goes up, we hope that all of you sitting in the theater will find a believable fantasy world. But I will see that effortless performance as the result of a great deal of solid, real-world, blue-collar collaborative effort.

For dancers, the process of working together doesn't look like what you may think of as collaboration—nothing's written down, and very little is spoken. If you stepped into my studio while I'm working with dancers, what you'd see is . . . dance. I don't tell, I show. Then they do. Something doesn't work? We try it again, look at it closely, make a modification. Dancers are smart, quick, and practical. Like intelligent people everywhere, they learn best by example. So do you.

Time's tight. You're busy. And there are people and organizations that need your talent and energy. Let's go.

- Aim high.
- Everything—and everyone—matters.
- There are no "details."
- If you do things right along the way, the end takes care of itself.

In his twenty-eight seasons as Duke University's basketball coach, Mike Krzyzewski has led his teams to three national championships, ten appearances in the Final Four, and eleven conference titles. Many coaches—and many CEOs—would pay dearly to know the secret of his success. Krzyzewski has no secret. Duke plays collaborative basketball—team basketball.

MIKE KRZYZEWSKI

Many coaches understand that the team approach is the best approach. But their players love to shoot, to play the playground game. Coach K operates on a higher plane. He tells his players: "The pass is still the best play, because our game is a game of connecting. If you lose the connection, you lose the spirit and then you lose your game." And his players believe him, and follow his teaching.

Mike Krzyzewski consistently succeeds because he applies the lessons of collaboration in every possible way:

—He personalizes his coaching. No two players, no two teams get the same approach.

—He notices every contribution to the team and points them out to the individual players as heroic acts. In South Africa, this concept is called *ubuntu,* or selflessness. The individual is exalted when the team is exalted; individual achievement diminishes the team.

—He makes few rules. The fewer the rules, the better he can deal individually with any problem.

—He involves the community. He calls Duke students "the sixth man" and sometimes talks with them before games, the better to direct their cheering.

—At the end of the season, he celebrates completion. Before the last game, the graduating seniors are introduced separately; after the game, the seniors take the court again to say good-bye. And then there's a banquet for the team. Finally, each graduating senior gets an individual video of his highlights.

Put those elements together, and you get a highly motivated group of players with a common mission. And although that mission is arduous, it's not grim: "You should live it right. You should live it together. You should live it shared. You should try to make one another better. You should get on one another if some people are not doing their part. You should hug one another when they are. You should be disappointed in a loss and exhilarated in a win. It's all about the journey."

Very simply, if you do it right at every step of the way, the result takes care of itself.

CHAPTER 2

Collaboration Is Second Nature

Collaboration probably started when our ancestors became hunter-gatherers and discovered it wasn't so easy to hunt or gather. Predators were bigger. They could run faster. And they could run longer. No way could early man quickly grow bigger or develop superior survival skills. So man figured out how to form tribes and find safety in numbers.

We've long forgotten how collaboration became a natural instinct. For most of us, in the dailiness of family life, collaboration is a learned habit. It's a welcome balance to the ego's incessant hunger for self-gratification. It's a recognition that there's more to life—more opportunity, more knowledge, more danger—than we can master alone. It's the building block of community. And because it's a balance to our self-absorption, it helps us see beyond ourselves to a universe full of people who are not all like us. It's a powerful tool for socialization and tolerance.

My childhood pointed me toward collaboration. I was born into a Quaker family in a small town in the Midwest farmland. As a toddler, I saw my grandparents along with other hardscrabble farmers and their families helping one another, and I learned there was real meaning in the way the community addressed its members as Friends.

My mother, Lecile Tharp, did her best to give me every advantage so that I could leave this difficult life. At eighteen months, I started learning music. I had perfect pitch, so, at age four, I began piano lessons. Soon I was entering competitions. By seven, I was beating kids twice my age. This kind of achievement demands considerable discipline. My mother required it—and I improved on her requirements. She prepared me to develop skills I could take out into the world and use with others. My daily schedule—which I copied, at age twelve, and saved—shows how completely she planned my days:

Monday

6:00–6:15: put practice clothes on

6:15–7:15: ballet

7:15–8:00: violin

8:00–8:30: get dressed, clean room, breakfast

8:30–9:00: go to school

9:00–3:00: school

3:00–3:15: go to violin

3:15–4:00: violin lesson

4:00–4:30: come home, snack, practice clothes

4:30–5:00: baton

5:00–5:30: tap

5:30–6:00: baton

6:00–7:00: kids' ballet

7:00–7:30: kids' baton

7:30–8:00: kids' tap

8:00–9:00: homework, shorthand

9:00–9:30: eat supper, get ready for bed

For the purposes of this book, the critical element is the hours between six and

eight P.M. Those two hours represented my first creative collaboration—each

night, as a dance teacher, I learned how to work with my twin brothers.

The twins spoke a language all their own. They looked—and acted—so alike that my parents couldn't tell them apart. Bonding came naturally to them; their struggle was to find separate identities. From six to eight, I learned to identify them as individuals through their movements; one liked to jump, one liked to turn. And they seemed to make progress in both dance and self-definition.

Not that I knew much about dance and baton. It didn't matter. What I didn't know I made up; then I'd drill the boys until they were ready to perform for me. Like teachers from the beginning of time, I got more out of these classes than my students.

And what I learned was life altering: I really enjoyed creating with other people. Specifically, I was fascinated by the idea that I could work with others to make something using only our bodies.

When I was seven, we moved to Southern California, hardly a cultural mecca in 1948. My mother still managed to find no end of classes for me to take. Ballet, violin, German—Mother wanted me to be prepared for everything and anything. While California had few instructors in each discipline, as soon as my mother decided that one was not up to her standards, she looked for a "better" teacher. It was very important that I study with "only the best."

I spent a year at Pomona College, which didn't offer enough dance to satisfy me, so I transferred to Barnard, which had dance classes and something even better: New York City's half dozen world-class dance companies. I was so determined—and programmed by Mom—that I had no hesitation about marching into the office of the head of dance at Barnard and saying, "I'm not going to take your classes, I'm going to study with Martha Graham and Merce Cunningham and Paul Taylor, and you're going to give me credits." And she said, "Sure, okay!"

I soaked up dance from every possible source, completely focused on figuring out what kind of dancer I wanted to be. I spent a year studying with Martha Graham, who was then the senior spokesperson of modern dance. I never expected her to be a mentor; I just went to her studio to watch and learn. I did everything she asked, absorbed every word she said, and moved aside deferentially on the narrow staircase when she was coming up. Graham was always very generous to me. When asked once who I was, she replied, "She's a rebel."

Paul Taylor was just removing himself from Martha Graham's universe when I came to his studio. I told him, "I'm going to sit up front and watch, and then I'll show you what I can do." I didn't give him a chance to turn me away. He saw I had some talent, so he put up with me for almost a year.

Merce Cunningham, a great dancer, was also a great teacher. And he had created a company of dancers who were also masterful teachers. Some were older, some were my age—and their greatest feature was that they could work together without losing their singularity. One of Merce's great strengths, both in his own dancing and in his choreography, was his openness to individual expression.

Each company represented the best of its generation. When I graduated from Barnard, I could have danced with any of them. Why didn't I?

I didn't lack for reasons. Graham's company was fraught with politics, which made it—a word I had just learned—dysfunctional. Taylor was young and impetuous, with the self-confidence of youth; he was both a dancer and a choreographer. While I enjoyed most of our work together, I never sensed a leading role in my future. And although creativity flowed like a river through Merce's company, his aesthetic was too abstract for me.

Of course there was a simpler reason—I wanted to choreograph my own dances and develop my own dancers. Read one way, that's the statement of a headstrong egotist. Read another way, it's a recognition that dance is hard work, that it requires a strong sense of dedication if you hope to achieve anything, and that, if you can't find others who are doing what you'd do, it's better to start your own enterprise and see who shows up.

Who showed up? Women. Not a big surprise. Much of the history of modern dance in America is the story of female choreographers leading all-female companies. Women often bond to form great teams. I recognize a common impulse when I read about women organizing to clear land mines in the Sudan or to harvest cactus for its healing properties in Morocco.

A dramatic example of the importance of collaboration for women comes from Bangladesh. In 1974, when famine struck, a young economics professor named

Muhammad Yunus saw that women were the poorest of the poor, earning as little as two cents a day. Their poverty was not of their making—they were simply excluded from the economic system, except, of course, as a source of cheap labor.

Yunus made a list of women who seemed like worthy borrowers. And, from his own pocket, he loaned forty-two women a total of $27. The women put up no collateral; he assumed every borrower was honest and would repay the loan. And he was right.

That's not feminism. It's practical idealism.

And so it was with me: I wanted to work with people who were like me, but also different at the same time. What we would share was an absolute sense of equality. No men, no music, no makeup. We were going to explore dance, we were going to dance for ourselves—we were the church of dance.

A clearly stated and consciously shared purpose is the foundation of great collaborations.

It helps to be young and struggling and short on money—in memoir after memoir, people seem to describe this period in their career as "the best years" of their life. I suspect, in most cases, that's true. But not because of the walk-up apartment and the budget meals. You are constructing your own opportunities. It's all about purpose and the clarity of ambition.

My first company was an extraordinary collective of women who were smart, talented, strong, and independent: Sara Rudner, Rose Marie Wright, Theresa Dickinson, Margery Tupling, Graciela Figueroa, and Sheila Raj. We began dancing together in 1966 and stayed together the next five years. Without pay. On the rare occasions when we were paid to perform, we split the fee seven ways. It may sound like the hardest path, but it had integrity. We worked as we saw fit. We needed no approvals, there were no union breaks, no one was watching.

Why did our collaboration work so well—and how could a start-up of yours maximize its chances of success?

The most important difference between my troupe and a failed start-up is discipline. We made a routine and we honored it, and if that was sometimes inconvenient, we sucked it up and got ourselves to rehearsals, on time and ready to work.

Collaboration doesn't flourish if people decide to get together "whenever." It's remarkably effective, however, when partners set a schedule and establish a routine—when working together becomes a habit.

> The sooner you establish a routine, the more smoothly your collaboration will advance.

How do you do this?

Often, with great difficulty.

Even with the best will in the world, creating a template for collaboration can be challenging. We have different senses of time. Our priorities are intensely personal. And our analysis of the workload ahead is invariably subjective.

The key to a workable routine?

First, make sure you really have agreed upon a common purpose. Amateur or professional—that distinction doesn't matter.

The first requirement of collaboration is commitment.

Some Japanese enterprises build in commitment with a decision-making process called *ringi.* It's a way of getting buy-in from everyone who will be involved in the consequences of a decision. It works this way: A document is created. And discussed. And changed until all the participants agree with it. Then everyone in the decision-making process affirms the agreement by placing the seal of their personal stamp on the document. An unnecessarily long, time-wasting process? Not at all, because once they have made their commitment, they don't return to reexamine and readjust it. They just execute, execute, execute.

Are you and your partners equally dependable?

Here's a paradox: Once you have confirmed that personal commitment, avoid all personal discussion as you make a schedule. That way, you won't get bogged down in the gossipy conversation that almost invariably turns scheduling into a negotiation. Avoid making that "special" routine you establish a thicket where you will surely get lost.

No need to reinvent the wheel. The schedule you want? It's known. It's whatever is the standard in the business or activity you're in. Start using it, then adjust if you need to.

Time changes everything, even a company of single-minded dancers. Our private lives—which we had kept neatly separated from our dancing—intruded, in the form of bills and families. I had a marriage and a son, and then the marriage ended, and I had a boy to support pretty much on my own. Something had to change. Very simply, we needed to earn a living.

When we did a piece called *Eight Jelly Rolls,* I thought I'd found a way to honor our art without selling out. For the first time, we used music. And costumes: backless tuxedos. I decreed that we would get our hair styled, and, to set an example, I went to Sassoon, then the hottest name in New York, and had my hair hacked off and shaped. Makeup also divided us: I put it on; some of the others refused.

Were we selling out? You could say that. I didn't see it that way. I thought: I'm taking on a persona, using this smoother surface as a veneer that will be pleasing to others. It didn't dilute my technique or get in the way of my real work; it just allowed an audience to see us as women they might like to know.

But *Eight Jelly Rolls* was not just a style change for us. It was a change in direction. For the first time, we were dancing not just for ourselves. We were taking on a new collaborator—an audience. And the audience responded, with cheering.

We'd broken the final barrier; we were now in collaboration with all the possible players—music, dancers, and audience. Ahead lay fresh opportunity.

I was lucky. When Bob Joffrey asked me if I'd like to make a ballet for his company, I was just thirty, still so young that my youthful brashness hadn't worn off. (It would soon be replaced by mid-thirties bluntness, which looked pretty much the same as youthful brashness, but never mind.) I wasn't so brash, however, that I forgot where I'd be working.

The Joffrey was the big time. And as a partner, Bob was ideal. A gifted choreographer, he was equally skilled as a company director. In both roles, he was welcoming and supportive of new talent.

It helps to have a champion.

Bob was the very model. He had worked with patronage as an artist himself for a large part of his career and understood—long before I did—that for me to succeed he would need to run interference. With his board and with his dancers. And he did that, free of agenda. He wanted a success for his company, but he knew that meant allowing me to give it a new definition.

My idea was to create a world for our two companies in a single piece. I searched for a metaphor and music. I found both in the Beach Boys. "Little Deuce Coupe" was one of their most popular songs. The car it celebrated—a two-door—could stand for our two top-of-the-line dance companies, coming together in one souped-up program. Maybe we'd achieve what the song described: "Comin' off the line when the light turns green / Well, she blows 'em outta the water like you never seen."

But my dancers and the Joffrey dancers had little in common. In our five years downtown, we had danced only in alternative spaces—parks, gymnasiums, museums. We'd never performed on a proscenium stage; until *Eight Jelly Rolls,* we'd never taken a curtain call. We'd given performances without audiences—once at 5:30 A.M. at the Cloisters, once in the rain—and we didn't care. If one of us got sick, we had no understudies, so we simply made a point of never getting sick! The Joffrey, in contrast, was a large, formal company, with a rich classical tradition, one whose technique didn't call for the kind of athletic strength that my choreography demanded.

Ultimately the most troublesome factor in this collaboration was . . . me. A female choreographer in the classical world was a rarity in the early seventies. In ballet, not many women were routinely telling men what to do—unless they were their mothers. Not surprisingly, some of the Joffrey's male dancers were unsure how to respond to my direction. I could say they didn't understand me. I could also say some of them weren't ready to take direction from a woman.

How did I break the standoff? When we started, I had said that I didn't want to impose Tharp style on Joffrey dancers. I had said I wanted a contrast; each dancer would be doing what he or she had been trained to do. Maybe the Joffrey dancers didn't believe it when I first said it. Maybe the second time they still saw it as a ploy. The real reason they came to trust me? Bob told them they had to.

If you want collaborators to "be themselves," you must accept them as they are.

The opening night of *Deuce Coupe* was great. Thrilling dancing, monumental reception, our first standing ovation. Looking out at row upon row of noisy, happy faces, I felt I was getting support for the idea of one dancer who could function in two heretofore alien worlds—the modern and the classical ballet.

Crossover technique. Once it was an ideal; now it was a possibility. Glamour, success, money? Happy thought. But not relevant. I considered the lines from one of the Beach Boys' songs we'd used—"Wouldn't it be nice to live together / In the kind of world where we'd belong." And I thought: The women and I, and now the Joffrey and I—these are good collaborations. Something's working.

How do you measure the vitality of your work environment? Look at your collaborative relationships. In a healthy environment, a good collaboration will extend your strengths.

- Really intense collaboration is a full-time job.
- Two single-minded partners with a shared interest can master entire disciplines and still be energetic enough to do original thinking.
- Creative disagreements between sympathetic collaborators spur new ideas.

When the Wright brothers were children, their father gave them a flying toy, powered by rubber bands. The actual toy didn't last long, but playing with it changed their lives.

Orville and Wilbur never considered working separately—they worked too well together. In terms of temperament, Orville was daring and Wilbur was visionary, but those

ORVILLE AND WILBUR WRIGHT

were unimportant distinctions. What mattered was what they had in common: astonishing mechanical skills and intellectual depth, buttressed by a willingness to work long hours without encouragement or recognition.

Wilbur and Orville began their collaboration as "The Wright Brothers" at twenty-two and eighteen, when they took parts from unrelated machines to build a printing press. A few years later, they bought bicycles and left the printing business to open a bike repair shop. Soon enough, they were building bicycles from scratch. Orville wanted to move on to build automobiles, but Wilbur said, "It would be easier to build a flying machine."

They eventually might have progressed from speedy, efficient bicycles to a flying machine, but their effort got a jump start in 1896, when Wilbur read about a German glider pilot's fatal accident. He began to muse about flight. He studied birds. Three years later, he asked the Smithsonian Institution to send him information on aeronautics.

The amount of work the Wrights did from 1900 to their first flight at Kitty Hawk, North Carolina, in 1903 is jaw-dropping. But then, so was their self-discipline. Their lives could hardly have been more monastic. They wore suits to their workshop. They never swore or worked on Sunday. As Wilbur put it: "My brother Orville and myself lived together, worked together, and in fact thought together."

Their challenges were vast. Not only did they need to perfect a plane that would stay aloft, they had to invent a small engine and a propeller. This required a willingness to plod on after failure and, at the same time, an ability to think big and fresh. They started, of course, with kites—versions of the childhood toy.

Their overarching big idea was to invent backward. They didn't build prototypes and then try to get them off the ground. They tried to fly first, then see what they needed to invent to stay aloft longer. In this, the closeness of their collaboration was key—they were able to think freely and propose anything without the fear of being judged.

Did they disagree? Often. "I love to scrap with Orv," Wilbur said. "Orv is such a good scrapper." But those scraps were all in the service of the project, not their sense of turf. They got several years beyond Kitty Hawk before Orville had occasion to remind his brother not to speak in the first person singular, as if he were the only inventor in the Wright family. Orville self-corrected immediately, and Wilbur didn't have to press the point.

For all their genius, they were eminently practical—they never flew together.

CHAPTER 3

Partnerships Challenge and Change Us

We are conditioned to think of partners as pairs. Start with Mom and Dad, move on to popular love songs and movies, end with our marriage vows. It's a romantic ideal: Two become one. So as a practical reality, let's look at collaboration with a single partner. We bounce ideas off another person. Then the other person volleys them back to us. That exchange makes us hear our ideas with new ears for the simplest of reasons—what our partners say is not a literal repetition of what we said.

People do not hear exactly what is said to them. And so, when they respond, we put our own spin on their answers. Even if they don't intend to, they raise questions and suggest other possibilities. Our ideas may blend to become a totally new entity.

The root of any collaboration is interchange—literally, change. Nothing forces change more dramatically than a new partnership.

Collaboration guarantees change because it makes us accommodate the reality of our partners—and accept all the ways they're not like us. And those differences are important. The more we can draw upon our partner's strengths and avoid approving our partner's weaknesses, the better that partnership will be.

Perhaps you recall the science class when you learned about Gregor Mendel and the breeding of yellow and green peas. When breeding blended the peas' best features, the result was "hybrid vigor"—stronger plants with better yields. "Hybrid vigor" is botany's idea of collaboration. In that genetic arithmetic, one and one don't make two.

You need a challenging partner. In a good collaboration, differences between partners mean that one plus one will always equal more than two.

In every obvious way, Mikhail Baryshnikov and I were opposites. The Russian and the midwesterner. Man and woman. The classically trained and the eclectically schooled. The result of this blend of opposites produced some innovative, exciting dancing that was different from what either of us could do on our own.

Baryshnikov had seen *Deuce Coupe* and decided that he wanted me to create a dance for him, which is just what the codirectors of American Ballet Theatre offered me late in 1975. This would be a challenge for any choreographer, and an even bigger one for a woman who worked outside the system.

I didn't know if we could work together. I had seen Baryshnikov perform classic nineteenth-century ballets, but the movement I was evolving, while grounded in a ballet vocabulary, was very different from what I saw him dancing onstage with American Ballet Theatre. So I said that I couldn't commit to a collaboration until I saw Baryshnikov in rehearsal.

This was a smart decision. Baryshnikov had defected from Russia only a year earlier; he was a megastar, beloved by audiences everywhere. If he were to appear in a piece that was not well received, he would be spared. All the blame would descend on the choreographer. I'd be eaten alive.

But you can't run from a challenge. And an opportunity—if there was one thing I would learn about Baryshnikov, it was that he wanted to try new things, that he was game for an experiment. For a choreographer obsessed with pushing the limits, nothing held greater appeal.

I deliberately arrived late at the ABT rehearsal, so I could watch Baryshnikov dance before I met him. I didn't anticipate his sense of drama—and fun. When rehearsal ended, without any warning, he turned a cartwheel and a somersault and landed right in front of me. He threw out his arms like a vaudeville performer and switched on his thousand-watt grin.

What do you say to charm like that—from someone you've never met? You gulp. You smile back. And you sign on for the ride.

Now, of course, you can do more research before your first meeting, and you can do it without alerting anyone or looking like a snoop. I mean, on the Internet. And I mean going deep, not settling for a first-screen Google search or a quick glance at Facebook or whatever is the social media watering hole of the moment. That's quite a luxury. Until recently, you had to hunker down in libraries and read microfilm to get more than surface information about anyone. And if you called someone who had useful information and your source happened to be a friend of the person you were researching, your query might not remain private—your source might pick up the phone and alert your subject. Awkward!

Henri Matisse regarded Paul Cézanne as "a sort of god of painting." Was his influence threatening—even dangerous? "Too bad for those without the strength to survive it," Matisse once said. "For my part, I have never avoided the influence of others."

That's how I felt about working with Baryshnikov—to have avoided the opportunity would have been cowardice.

Movement was a great communication zone for us. I spoke no Russian. His English was minimal. We mostly communicated through movement. If I needed to talk to explain a point, his language circuits would shut down and he'd go . . . inside. We needed a translator but there was none.

A language barrier? Not really. We had a common language—we were dancers with similar work habits. We were both used to technique class in the morning and then rehearsal following that. Daily. Annually. That is ultimately what allowed us to work together.

Baryshnikov had other performing commitments, so we rehearsed as much as we could while he was in New York. When he was away, I did what I could by myself. I added some music by Joseph Lamb, a prominent ragtime composer. I introduced a single prop—a bowler hat. And I worked with the other dancers in the ballet. Meanwhile, on the road, Baryshnikov showed that he had fully signed on to this collaboration by rehearsing diligently on his own.

When Baryshnikov returned, I had the first full cast run-through for the ballet. There was some confusion: Is my entrance upstage or downstage of that exit? Wait, someone else is on during my variation! But we weathered this first session very well. Watching the dancers' faces when Baryshnikov performed told me all I needed to know—we had come up with something new. We had respected our differences and then analyzed them to find new ways of recombining.

If I make this sound like a nearly frictionless process, it wasn't. There are uncomfortable moments during any collaboration, and Baryshnikov and I had our share of misunderstandings and disagreements. But we never stopped reaching out to each other—the adventure of a new challenge encouraged us to trust the new and to take yet another step.

"It is not the strongest species that survives, nor the most intelligent," Charles Darwin wrote in 1859. "It is the one that is most adaptable to change."

A great partnership is a lab where change happens every day.

Opening night of *Push Comes to Shove*. Barshynikov entered, a dazzling rake with a hat. He danced. He circled. He ran his fingers through his hair. Then he was aloft. Talk about a high—this was a record breaker. He'd honored his compact with the audience; they got what they came for. And he went on to give them so much more than what they expected in the form of many surprises.

For Baryshnikov it was an artistic triumph—it showed he could dance anything, classical or modern or even the as yet unnamed. He'd forced audiences to expand their idea of him. In a word, he'd freed himself.

For me, the triumph was just as big. Not only had I revealed a great dancer's ability to go beyond the moves and music that made him famous, I had done it in a way that hadn't endangered his artistic reputation. And because "everybody" came to see Baryshnikov, my world expanded: Milos Forman would ask me to choreograph his next film, *Hair*.

Baryshnikov and I worked together again shortly after the *Push* premiere. For an ABT gala we made a duet to the music of Frank Sinatra. Two things were unexpected about this little piece. The partnering between the two of us was totally unconventional—neither balletic nor ballroom—and Baryshnikov never left the ground even once. Baryshnikov was, of course, among other things, a sublimely coordinated athlete. His speed, maneuverability, and power were unmatched, the height of his jump breathtaking. So when we held this jump back in order to show another dimension of his talent, many felt we were mean-spirited. We were roundly booed. That response was painful at the time; still this duet gave me the opportunity to begin really thinking about partnering.

Talk about the beginner and the Stradivarius. While I had structured partnered movement in both *Deuce Coupe* and *Push,* lifting, dipping, and swirling are not the skills that one ordinarily associates with an all-female dance ensemble. With Baryshnikov, I had begun to investigate partnered dance moves from the inside out.

After two more small ballets for Baryshnikov and ABT, I was hired in 1985 to create a dance sequence for a movie called *White Nights*. The idea I was asked to develop was to showcase the film's main characters, played by Baryshnikov and Gregory Hines, in what was to look like a rehearsal studio in Leningrad. The contrasts were compelling. One great ballet star, one fabulous tap dancer. One compact blond, the other lanky dark. One trained at the Kirov Ballet over the course of eight demanding years to a point of near-classical perfection, the other brought up as one half of a brothers' act on the vaudeville route.

Where to begin? Always, with what the dancers most enjoy. And here Baryshnikov and Hines were remarkably alike. Both were fantastic jumpers, with fabulous reflex speed; they were both rhythmically sophisticated and brilliantly coordinated. In this partnership, they were both egoless—they knew how good they were and how little they had to prove to one another.

Their best commonality: Each was the other's biggest fan. What a difference that makes! They were never competitive—playing around, Greg taught Misha a time-step and Misha taught Greg an open pirouette, but they never thought to wear each other's shoes when the cameras rolled.

This made my job embarrassingly easy. Not only because both men were consummate artists, but because of the genuine respect each had for the other. There was an easy willingness between them to bring their best to the table, to take any ideas I might throw their way, and to share the unfamiliar blend with the cameras as though they had been living with it all their lives.

Ours was a strange Mendelian mix—three very different foreigners shooting in London for Leningrad—but it had great creative magnetism. Often I felt my contribution was just as an interface.

I worked with both men separately, finding ways to feature them within their individual virtuosities and realms. But I also transferred some of my personal style to them for moments that had them dancing in unison. Ultimately, it was this outsider element that bound them together.

And that was my role in another unlikely collaboration, with the championship figure skater John Curry. I had never even been on a pair of skates, and when we began to work together, John preferred I keep it that way—he didn't want the responsibility of propping me up. Thus my role was relegated to the outsider standing on the edge of the rink and asking him to try this, try that.

For many skating aficionados, John was the consummate practitioner of his art, as elegant in his sphere as Baryshnikov was in his. Clearly, I would not be improving his form during our project, but I could think up some outrageous propositions that he could absorb, making it possible for him to surprise and even shock some of the official world of skating when the piece was performed in Madison Square Garden.

As for me, I learned ways of extending movement from one place to another that would never have occurred to me had I not been able to transpose myself into this amazing artist, to feel the innumerable hours he had trained, drilled, and practiced from one inside edge to the other outside edge and back, carefully tracing his patterns into the ice.

Ultimately, the debt I owe all my partners can never be returned, but only acknowledged with the greatest gratitude.

- A collaboration may not be what it appears.
- Chance is an unseen collaborator.
- Uncredited collaborators are often key to successful outcomes.

Fred and Ginger. We don't need their last names to know them. They're part of our cultural DNA—the movies they made together in the 1930s have immortalized them as one of the greatest dance teams ever filmed.

Fred Astaire and Ginger Rogers were sublime as partners. But they weren't really collaborators. When it came to creating the dances that made Fred and Ginger into icons of dance in film, Astaire's collaborator was a young choreographer named Hermes Pan.

FRED ASTAIRE AND HERMES PAN

This wasn't a matter of clashing personalities but of competence. Astaire had grown up as a doubles act with his sister. At first, he wasn't pleased to be teamed with Rogers. "Ginger had never danced with a partner before," he said. "She faked it an awful lot. She couldn't tap and she couldn't do this and that . . ." But she worked hard—and, on camera, made work look like fun. Astaire soon had to admit they were well matched: "After a while everyone else who danced with me looked wrong."

The cocreator of the dances that Astaire and Rogers seemed to be inventing on the spot was Hermes Pan. Has any dancer been better named?

The son of the Greek consul in Nashville, he was a dance-crazed kid who fled Tennessee when he was just fourteen, already good enough to be hired in the chorus of a musical comedy in New York. By twenty, he was an assistant dance director for Broadway. At twenty-two, he was working in Hollywood.

Pan was a twenty-three-year-old assistant dance director when he met Astaire on the set of *Flying Down to Rio*. A song in that movie, "The Carioca," worked well with the kind of dancing Pan had seen African Americans do in Tennessee. He was trying out some of those steps when Astaire noticed.

"Could I do that?" Astaire asked.

"Sure," Pan said. "You do everything else."

In that moment, Astaire acquired a teacher, a partner, a commentator—and a much-needed collaborator. Typically, he and Pan would begin working together a month before filming. They'd "fool around," looking for a routine to reveal itself. A few steps would emerge. "For the first two weeks, I play Rogers," Pan explained to an interviewer. "I know how she dances and what she expects from Astaire. I'm her reverse side."

Eventually Rogers was called in—to watch. Then Pan, playing Astaire, would teach her the routine. As for Astaire and Rogers, they had time to perfect their dancing—each number might be shot as many as forty times.

The audience saw only Fred and Ginger. But Astaire's real collaborator was just off camera, five feet from the dancers.

CHAPTER 4

Working with a Remote Collaborator

It was my son, Jesse, who suggested that I do an evening of dance and music with Billy Joel. As a songwriter and performer, Jesse said, Billy had an uncanny ability to reach the mass audience. Many of his songs got your feet moving. Many of his ballads had women and men alike misting up. And his music was big—there was rage in it, and courage, and tragedy, and the triumph of sheer survival.

But could the poet laureate of Long Island—and many points west—lure audiences to Broadway? I listened. I thought I saw a theme, one already familiar to me: the emotional effect of the Vietnam War. That was the spine of *Hair*. But Milos Forman was at least a decade too early with that movie—the feelings of the American audience were still too raw, positions too entrenched. Now, though, perhaps we could deal with the war's human costs on a generation of American men.

I'd never met Billy. And I wasn't about to pitch him without a calling card. So I gathered six performers—who would go on to play the leading roles in *Movin' Out*—and made a twenty-minute video. Only then did I invite Billy to my apartment to see how his songs might be the centerpiece of a dance-powered Broadway musical. As soon as the video ended, he signed on.

If you want a successful first meeting, preparation pays. Get everything on your side before you say hello.

When you're collaborating with a megastar who's already written the music you're going to use, there's no way to have an equal collaboration. As a practical matter, there was no reason to drag him into the production. This was a collaboration with Billy's music, not with Billy. With one important assist: Billy has a staff that can answer every question about orchestration and production. If I did the work and Billy did the publicity, our show had a chance.

This was a smart division of labor. I'm not ambivalent about the press, but experience has taught me to be cautious. Billy is an outsize, exuberant personality. He's a pro at smiling for the cameras and delivering a smart quip. In this relationship, no one would be fighting him for the media spotlight.

The production had bumps. In Chicago, I agreed with audiences that the show needed work. Those audiences were my most useful collaborators. Without them, I'd have been pretty much on my own, for I was wearing three hats: writer, choreographer, director.

And then, to my great relief, I got extraordinary support from Billy, who was even more of a mensch than I'd thought. He never ducked an interview. He gave parties for the cast and friends. He offered some helpful suggestions for the show. And, at a crucial moment, he showed up—big-time.

At one point during rehearsals, it was making me crazy that so many of our dancers were riding to the theater on their motorcycles. One cab door opens, one tire skids on an oil slick—suddenly you've got a cast member on the in-jured list. But there was nothing I could do to keep the dancers off their bikes. A Broadway director may be all-powerful in the theater, but only until she runs into union power.

And then suddenly my worst fears were realized. When it came, the accident was much worse than I could have imagined—there was a long night in the hospital, and in the morning, William Marrie was dead. I was heartbroken. And furious. I called an early-morning meeting. "I can't *order* you to stop riding your motorcycles," I told the cast. "But I am *telling* you to stop. I *need* you to stop. Until the production ends, *no more bikes*."

Billy didn't have to be at this gathering. But he hauled into town for it. And then he did something really powerful. Billy loves motorcycles. Not just to collect. To ride—New Yorkers have learned not to be surprised when a guy parks his bike, pulls off his helmet, and there's Billy Joel. But at the cast meeting, Billy announced that he, too, would stay off his bike for the run of the show.

More than 90 percent of Broadway shows don't last a year. *Movin' Out* was enthusiastically received, ran for three years, toured for several more, and made investors extremely happy. It did everything I'd hoped for. And came with a bonus—as people were filing out after the show, more than once I'd hear, "I came for Billy, but those dancers . . ."

Bob Dylan is charming, smart, funny—and, like Billy Joel, very busy. When he called to suggest that we collaborate on a dance musical, it was clear that I would be filling in most of the dotted lines. And that was a blinking yellow light, for Dylan's catalogue is massive. Before I started looking through it in search of a dramatic thread, I thought to prove to myself—and to reassure us both—that his songs were danceable.

I identified some songs and developed a few moves. When we met, I turned on the music and gave Dylan a demonstration—a few minutes of "Sugar Baby."

"You have to practice to do that," said Dylan.

"No more than you," I parried.

"I didn't know anybody could move that fast to my music. How do you do it?"

The secret, I said, was in the time signature. Say his song's meter is a heavy 2/4. I make each beat a triplet. This gives a lightness to music that can sound very heavy.

"I don't understand everything you are saying, but I trust you," he said.

The Times They Are A-Changin' was the product of one year of research and preparation and another year and a half of casting, rehearsing, and workshops. Early in 2007, we were closing in on two years of preparation when Dylan came down to San Diego for a private performance at the Old Globe Theatre. He arrived early. He paid close attention. He gave his blessing. And off he went.

As it happened, I was still in San Diego when I got a call from the Miami City Ballet. Its founder and director, Edward Villella, was creating a gala evening and had commissioned Elvis Costello to write a new score. He wanted me to do the choreography.

I always choose my collaborators—except when I don't. And when I don't have the luxury of choice, I'm just the same as the employee who's assigned to a team at a new company or the worker on a new crew. I have a decision to make: Get along or leave.

Elvis Costello came along at an interesting time. Dylan had been an absentee collaborator. But Elvis sent word that he "wanted to write new music." And Elvis had a track record that proved he could write for ballet.

He'd burst on the English music scene in 1977 with a terrific, energetic album called *My Aim Is True.* He had a string of hits; his band was tight; as a wry lyricist, he has almost no equals. But Elvis is more than a New Wave perennial with a knack for the 2:45 pop song. He has range. Look at his collaborations—from Paul McCartney to the Kronos Quartet to Burt Bacharach. The evidence was voluminous: Elvis would try anything.

I had danced to several of his songs over the years for fun in the studio and had found a tartness to his harmonies and a sensuality in the rhythms. Ominous, complex, dark—three more words to describe the kind of energy that came into my movements when I danced to his music. As an artist, Costello was obviously restless; he liked to push boundaries and mix musical influences. "Do not go where the path may lead, go instead where there is no path and leave a trail," Ralph Waldo Emerson wrote. This seemed a sentiment Costello might recognize. I had listened to music he'd written for a ballet and a symphonic work, and I felt he would be up to the challenge of a new dance collaboration.

Still, although my contract with MCB was only for the dance, I added some music stipulations: a deadline for the first draft of the music and another for the completed score. Why did I insist on those deadlines? Committing to make a dance with music you not only haven't heard but that hasn't yet been written is a gamble. While I have worked this way on films, where the score almost always shows up last, in Miami I wanted to guarantee myself revision time before the ballet's premiere.

But it's more than that.

With the best intentions in the world, things go wrong. You need to protect yourself. And the less well you know your collaborator, the more protection you need.

If you can negotiate a respectful, responsible exit—in essence, a prenup— before you need to think about an exit strategy, do it. So don't be shy about speaking up early: that is, before you start. You never have more power than when someone wants to hire you and you are a heartbeat from signing on.

I had one more reason to be careful. Elvis Costello is a celebrity, and a celebrity is made of many people, usually a team—press agents, public relations people, lawyers, managers. These folks wish to look after not only their star but also their own paychecks. The conglomerate they form is the proverbial 800-pound gorilla.

If you are not in the entertainment industry, you may not be working frequently with people who carry this gorilla on their backs, so let's redefine a celebrity as anyone in your life who's on the A-list and thinks of you as someone on the B-list—that is, anyone who has authority and power over you. The moral for you is the same as the moral for me: Do not be intimidated. Ultimately, you're working with just one person.

Of course, as soon as I met Elvis Costello, I felt I'd been worried over nothing.

In person, Elvis Costello is a lovable bear of a man with a tiny gap between his front teeth. He wears cowboy boots and a stiff black straw hat and his smile suggests his sly Irish wit. At our first meeting there is no posturing or gossip. Elvis couldn't be a nicer guy. He's a worker: authentic, straight to the point, smart. And organized? He takes notes on his laptop.

That first meeting was a kind of mutual pitch session. In our case, Elvis had brought some of his older songs that he wanted to reference in our score, as well as a couple of sketches for new music. I'd sampled the full range of his work, and I'd edited a rough video of some of my old work synced to cues from his songs. All of this I considered "kindling" to get the fire going.

As we say our good-byes, Elvis promises to have a scratch track for me to take to Miami for my spring rehearsal period. We already seem to have solved many of the ballet's problems and fallen into collaborator heaven.

So far, so good. Maybe the stars do align when you're older and wiser.

With Elvis off to compose, I turn to my other collaborators on this project, beginning with Edward Villella. At New York City Ballet in the 1960s and 1970s, he was a great dancer at a great time in the company's history, and was a talent crucial to both Balanchine and Robbins. Plagued by injuries, he retired in his prime. Today he's energetically developing dancers, passing the knowledge on as one of the only artistic directors in all of American dance to have founded a company and still be with it. Miami is lucky to have him.

Eddie's a great partner for me because he completely understands that the old dance choice—are you a ballet dancer or a modern dancer?—is a false one. Ever since my success with *Deuce Coupe* at the Joffrey, I've pushed to merge the styles in a practical and inclusive way. Eddie's obviously sympathetic to this; I wouldn't be in Miami if he weren't.

Ordinarily I would bring an assistant I know and trust, but in Miami, I decide not to do this. My assistant will be Crista Villella, Eddie's daughter. This is her first new ballet, but she's grown up with these dancers, is bright and committed, and has inherited her dad's energy gene. One evening I watch her conduct a children's rehearsal for *The Nutcracker*—she's a strong, clear manager, sympathetic with the kids without compromising her authority. And there's a bonus: Crista has rehearsed some of my old pieces in Miami City Ballet's repertoire. She has a sense of my priorities. She'll be helpful when I need to match dancers with roles.

In Miami, I may have memorized the names of the dancers, but I don't really know them. During a class or rehearsal, things happen fast. If you're taking your own notes, you're likely to end up with a sheaf of scrawled gibberish. And then what do you do when suddenly a dancer is injured and an extra rehearsal is called in a second studio so the replacement can get up to speed?

An assistant gives you someone to bounce an idea off, get an impression from. In effect, an assistant doubles your rehearsal hours. A wink at the end of an exhausting day tells you that you've still got fifteen more good rehearsal minutes. And, over time, if the assistant learns the new work well, you can be assured that the ballet will get up even if you are hit by a bus.

In any collaboration, assistants are as valuable as you allow them to be. Treat assistants with respect and you will gain valuable collaborators.

The care and feeding of assistants has always been important to me— unfortunately this is far from a universal priority. Why some people brutalize their assistants and the assistants of others, demanding special and instant attention, is a mystery to me.

That assistant you're tempted to scream at may be extravagantly talented. And ambitious. And promotable. Someday that assistant could be the boss— someone who can really help you, someone you might actually need.

What goes around, comes around—assistants live for that moment. So, if you're smart, will you.

You can't keep secrets or personal quirks from your assistant. I tell Crista right off: I am demanding; I expect you to be at least as early as I am to rehearsal (hey, if you aren't early, you're late), to know the scores and to calibrate the rehearsal audio, noting music entry points for all the dance phrases, to oversee the studio video, to work late editing the day's tape, to have prepared any phrases that will be introduced to the dancers in the next day's rehearsal. And there's more: to be enthusiastic, willing, and energetic. To gauge when in a rehearsal to speak and when not, when to subjugate your opinion to what you know is the plan and when to speak frankly if the plan is veering off course.

Daunting requirements. Crista assures me she will do her best. No doubt she will. But we won't really be able to tell how well I have done my job with Crista until she's in charge on her own.

And don't forget this. A relationship that was simple—in my case, between the dancers and me—becomes compound when the assistant is in the middle. And your collaboration will become complex when the assistant begins to deal with the scheduling of both your time and that of your coworkers. Suddenly, where there were only dancers in the studio, there are now board members, production teams, promotional people, and administrative staff with their own sets of demands for you and your assistant. Just keep going.

My final collaborators: the dancers.

One of the first things I do in Miami is watch Eddie give a thorough barre, obviously one that his dancers have done hundreds if not thousands of times. But no one is bored—they all understand that these challenges must be re-addressed every day. As the dancers come to the center, I can see they're strong from the rigor of the discipline. When I look at gorgeous women and elegant men like these, their limbs well prepared for the tasks ahead, I always feel the same emotion: enormous gratitude to the trainers, coaches, and teachers who have lovingly groomed their charges, day after day, year after year. They build my resources. Thanks to these silent and unnamed collaborators, I stand a shot of getting something done.

It's said that we burn almost a third of our daily calories in our eyes. Looking, blinking, concentrating—at the end of a long day of watching dancers rehearse, I'd believe in that percentage. And in the first stage of a collaboration, I try to watch without preconceptions. An older dancer comes into view. Frail in appearance, her concentration is intense. Next to her, every piece of clothing carefully folded and patted into place, is a younger dancer, cool and pulled together. Here's a well-proportioned man, agile, efficient, fluid; obviously very intelligent. On another barre are two sets of twins who could supply endless confusion in any cast. And the Cubans. They seem to hang together, but then most everyone in the room speaks Spanish.

The first moment in a studio with excellent dancers is always exciting. I anticipate the challenges to come with real enthusiasm. Will we find the common purpose that allows us all to buy into a unifying vision?

The studio's a happy place. I am pushing hard, perhaps getting greedy; I need to be wary of injuring the dancers. But the new work comes very quickly. None of Elvis's new music has arrived yet, so I begin making material on some of his old songs.

During the second week, I ask the dancers to bring in their favorite Latin dance music. I do this for two reasons. One, when they move to music they love, they're loose and at their best. And there's also the psychological reason: A good way for the dancers to feel invested in the work is to make it clear that you actually care what they think. I want them to know that I'll let them contribute, that they can modify my dream without offending me, because my vision is such a big target that even if they move it to the left or the right I can still see it.

In *Butch Cassidy and the Sundance Kid,* I'm fond of a scene that comes late in the film, when Butch and Sundance flee to Bolivia. They try to get hired as payroll guards, so, naturally, the boss wants to know if Sundance is a good shot. "Can you hit anything?" he asks. Sundance's laconic reply: "Sometimes." So the boss tosses up a book of matches. "Hit that," he orders. Sundance shoots—and misses. The boss is disgusted. Sundance asks, "Can I move?" The boss shrugs, tosses another small target. Sundance crouches. Spins. Shoots. Every bullet hits. "I'm better when I move," he says.

In any collaboration, there is no one way. Go with whatever works.

Considering the timetable in Miami—two weeks now in the spring with the dancers and five more in the fall, five hours a day, 175 hours total—I'm reasonably calm. I know that sounds like a lot of rehearsal time. It's not. It's a drop in the bucket. But the dancers are doing so well I decide we can afford a midway approach between weeks of improvisation and a work completed before I have even begun rehearsals.

Just one problem. No music yet from Elvis Costello.

And now comes the surprise: Elvis misses the first deadline.

Even worse: Though I am sympathetic—Elvis has a wonderful new family with understandable complications—he says he won't be able to deliver even a rough working score until after the first rehearsal period is over.

I'm devastated. Elvis promised me at the very least some new melodies when I was in Miami. Now he suggests I use the rough track he'd brought to our first meeting. I use this very preliminary music as a reference, but I also mix in some songs by the Gipsy Kings, always a great dancing fallback.

I'm also *not* devastated. Elvis is a pro. Surely there will still be time before the second rehearsal period for him to deliver.

But Elvis misses his second deadline as well. Why? He's on the road, opening for Bob Dylan! In an e-mail, he explains that he is working on the ballet in a trailer next to Dylan's, but "it's hard to keep 'All Along the Watchtower' out of the score." I e-mail back: "I know what you mean."

Elvis isn't a slacker. If anything, he's doing too much—juggling his family, various administrators, managing schedules, his touring. This ballet program puts one too many balls in the air for him.

Ever the gent, Elvis does the gentlemanly thing and offers to end the collaboration. I don't want this. Losing Elvis would be devastating to the company, which had already done an enormous amount of fund-raising for the project, a lot of it, I am sure, based on his name and reputation. I tell him, "We need to make this work—any way that's good for you."

Elvis agrees.

That's when our collaboration became virtual.

61

Things change. You've got to be prepared to accept the inevitable roadblocks and find new tools you never thought you'd have to use.

Like e-mail. Because that's what virtual collaboration means for most of us—e-mail, with attached documents or videos or MP3s.

The Internet is the greatest literacy project since Gutenberg invented movable type in the 1400s. It makes everyone who uses it a better reader—and a more effective writer. And it accomplishes this in a form that's become so natural, many of us don't even think of it as writing.

Writing effective e-mail, like everything else, is all about habit. The scale of the collaboration doesn't matter. Only the content does, and the clarity with which it's presented.

As in all writing, personality counts. You're not sending an order for widgets to a scanner that will convert words into action. You're writing to a person. You want something. You want to do something. You want to offer something.

This requires a modicum of personality. Maybe a little more. No need to quash your humanity.

A friend who likes his e-mail collaborators to give him what he wants, first gives them something he thinks they want: easy-to-read mail. He believes the e-mail form is too wide, that your eye doesn't want to go that far to the right. So he uses only half the line and writes what looks like blank-verse poetry. He's busy and writes many e-mails a day, but he never fails to design the communication. And he tries never to hit SEND without inserting at least one flash of his personality.

People react warmly to the sight of his name in their in-box.

Still, even the warmest, most precise e-mail is no substitute for a face-to-face meeting.

It's far from the ideal way for a choreographer to work with a composer.

So why didn't I bail?

Call it stubbornness. Call it foolishness. Call it honor. I've had the contractual right to leave a collaboration many times, and I've never used it. There never seemed reason; I've often felt inconvenienced, but I've never felt insulted or disrespected. The film director Peter Weir once remarked, "You can make the deal or you can make the movie"—that is, you can take the time to negotiate a contract that's lovely as a work of legal prose, or you can get on with the real work of making real art in the real world. I'm with him. Even at the risk of failure.

Collaborative projects offer tutorials in reality. And that tutorial always presents the unexpected.

At a lecture, Shunryu Suzuki, one of the Zen masters who brought Buddhist practice to the United States, was asked to summarize Buddhism in a sentence.

The audience laughed at the impossibility of that challenge. But the Zen master had a ready answer. "Easy," he said. "Everything changes."

That is the challenge. Left to our own devices, we all tend to plan in a way that would produce one result. Then we add a collaborator—and the board changes. Between us, can we create a new way to play our new game?

So, okay, Elvis and I will work long-distance. As it happens, this won't be the first time for me. Late in the sixties, dancing on a farm in upper New York State, I acquired a thirdhand video system in the hopes of being able to continue working with two dancers—one in Uruguay, the other in India— who had lost their green cards. And in the ensuing four decades, I have documented my career in video diary form, in part to record my evolution as a dancer and choreographer, in part to have valuable material on hand, much as composers might go to their trunk for a tune they have never used but have never forgotten.

I'm glad I started recording all those years ago. I'm not a technology buff, but these experiences—plus working on five feature films and many hours of television—have given me facility with editing techniques. It's nice to have that skill, especially now, when cable and satellite systems allow anyone to be virtually present.

Elvis, feeling bad, undertakes a herculean effort. He sends e-mails and MP3s at all hours of the night and day from every time zone on earth as he squeezes work into a touring schedule that already is leaving very little time for his family. I receive segments almost daily and try to feel the flow of the ballet from them. I spend hours syncing and cueing, editing my Miami rehearsal video to Elvis's new music.

Using Final Cut Pro (a video editing program), MP3s, and e-mail, I create a virtual dance of sorts. Using the phrases created in Miami, some of them originally set to the Gipsy Kings, I reedit the dance so it's synced with the new music from Elvis.

By the time I arrive in Miami for the next rehearsal period, Elvis, amazing man that he is, has kept his word—he's delivered a synthesizer score for the entire ballet. I proceed to invent new material for the second half of the ballet while Crista doubles back to rehearse the dancers with material from the spring and a mile-long list of cuts, loops, and juxtaposed phrases that I'd edited in New York.

It can be done. You can have a virtual collaboration with a partner who's just . . . not there. This is not, however, an unequivocal endorsement of virtual collaboration.

There were some problems—starting with e-mail.

As everyone who uses it knows, e-mail encourages a kind of terse, immediate answer—yes! no!—that doesn't supply any context below the surface to explain what your response really means. It flattens intellectual complexity, amps up emotion. It's great for business—yes! no!—but hostile to art. Elvis did much better with this distance correspondence form than most. Along with the musical attachment, he sent chatty and informative messages.

As for using video, a good solution in one situation turned out to be not successful in another. Watching a dance video, I miss context. I miss process. I miss the ability to ask the dancer—right now, please—to try it another way. And I resent the pressure to respond immediately—machines do not afford the time for a lot of stewing.

So I'm of two minds about virtual collaboration. I fear that technology can force us to move too quickly for our good, establishing its own world and pushing us to make decisions—yes! no!—before we're ready. And I don't like that every technological compromise is compromise only on the human side; we adjust to the computer, never the other way around. So there are times for me when face-to-face is still required.

It is always a very good thing to visit artists in their studios, scientists in their labs, administrators in their offices. Once you have a sense of the lair, it is easier to project an emotional component into distance collaborations.

My first distance collaboration was with composer Donald Knaack, aka The Junkman. Had I not visited Don in his Vermont shop where he builds the recycled trash constructions he plays on, I would not have been able to make either sense or revisions out of his daily FedEx recordings that came from Vermont to my New York studio as we created *Surfer at the River Styx*.

Miami. Three days before the premiere. Elvis arrives.

He goes directly to the orchestra rehearsal and begins to appreciate some of the challenges he will face. The string section is much too small to deliver a big "Hollywood" sound; pushed, the sound system begins generating awesome (but not in a good way) feedback. Some of the players in the Latin band are not quite up to the music's difficulty and some tweaking will be required.

I go to the music rehearsal so I can hear the score as the audience would, but I remind myself to stay uninvolved and to leave Elvis to his work.

I can't emphasize this idea enough. Getting involved with your collaborator's problems almost always distracts you from your own. That can be tempting. That can be a relief. But it usually leads to disaster.

My decision not to step in here is really the biggest help I can give Elvis. With lights, costumes, and injuries, I have issues enough. I may be the director of the entire program, but live bands are not my domain. I can only slow Elvis down or, worse, get in his way. If you take away a single piece of advice from this chapter, here is the one to remember: Don't sign on for more problems than you must. Resist the temptation to involve yourself in other people's zones of expertise and responsibility. Monitor troublesome situations if you need to, but don't insert yourself unless you're running out of time and a solution is nowhere in sight. In short, stifle your inner control freak.

The dress rehearsal is a disaster. Dancers miss their entrance cues, some are unhappy with aspects of their costumes, and two of the leading men are injured, though they're determined to perform.

Good.

Good? Yes, because it's a tradition that a terrible last rehearsal guarantees a good opening night. Of course I don't count on this, so I fester quietly. Tradition also says that leaders remain calm under stress. That is a canard. I have seen very few instances of this in my career, but I try to set an example. When the tension mounts, I work out even more than usual, hoping that, as it so often does, exercise will drain anxiety.

In the film business, right after a movie finishes shooting, there's a gathering called a wrap party (as in, "It's a wrap," meaning that it's finished). In my world, I see opening nights as a wrap party—that is, the ballet is finally wrapped in its costumes, its lights, its hair and makeup, and its full live orchestration. It's a momentary triumph of theatricality over "real" life, and it's to be cherished.

Opening night, ready or not, is also cause for a gala party, a celebration that is—as in Miami—a mainstay of the company's fund-raising for the year. Usually I am miserable; I have to work hard to suppress a scowl. It's not that I don't like social events—though I don't—but that I am in a postpremiere snit about the performance. I want to scream: "The thing is not what you saw tonight!" But no one wants to hear that—certainly none of my collaborators. So I struggle to get over myself.

Opening night—or any ceremonial event at the completion of a collaboration—is not about one individual. It's the celebration of a group endeavor. And that means, if you're the team leader, you want to be sure everyone on the team gets acknowledged.

It's easy to do that tonight. The dancers loved Isaac Mizrahi's costumes, with their hibiscus colors. Elvis Costello brought in a score the musicians enjoyed playing and the cast enjoyed performing. The ovations at the end of the show told us the audience liked us.

Party time is, for me, a continuation of the performance; it's a celebrity star turn. Elvis and I go round to each table, thanking patrons, having photos taken.

I'm delighted to see him enjoying this moment. For the year and a half this project has been in his life, he's been a performer, a songwriter, a serious composer, a husband with a very successful wife—and a new father. To this list add extremely gracious party guest.

The ballet? This program would go on to produce the largest box office sales in the company's history. But when a gala audience is presented with both a new dance and an intimate moment with a star, the intimate moment will win every time. Not the music. Not the dance. This is where the celebrity factor pays off.

Elvis knows this. So when the band begins to play "My Funny Valentine"—a song that he's recorded so well it's now one of his signature numbers—he spontaneously takes over the microphone, rewarding the ballet's patrons for their support with a very generously given performance that few others will ever experience: Elvis Costello singing just for them and very close up.

As for me, my reward came in the form of an e-mail from my assistant Crista:

Miami loved *Nightspot*. On Sunday the whole audience stood before the curtain even went down! I have never seen that before down here. There was applause throughout the whole show, and it was standing room only. We never sell out like that. We have all grown as artists because of you. Many people I have talked to (my friends, parents of *Nutcracker* kids, students) said that *Nightspot* was the coolest ballet that we have ever done. We here in Miami couldn't be more thrilled and we couldn't love you more. Crista. PS. Second cast will be totally awesome.

When the second cast—the backup team, the bench—is raring to go and fully prepared to take over, you know the collaborative relationship was deep and powerful. This is the ultimate compliment.

- A willingness to try for the unknown can be a strong bond.
- Only those who go too far know how far they can go.

It's always easier when collaborators start with the same blank slate, even if they don't know how they want to color it in. That was my experience with David Byrne.

The oddity of our collaboration was that we both lived in New York, had much in common, and yet didn't know each other. We did, however, both know Bill Graham, and Bill shrewdly put us together.

Dance and music are so linked that it was probably inevitable I'd become a friend of the rock promoter who created rock 'n' roll meccas in the 1960s at the Fillmore East and West. I met Bill in the late seventies, when rock had become less of a movement and more of a business. Three of

DAVID BYRNE

the greatest talents Bill championed—Janis Joplin, Jimi Hendrix, and Jim Morrison—had lived hard and died young.

But Bill was always looking forward, and a musician he especially liked was David Byrne. He thought there were collaborative possibilities for us, so he arranged for us to meet.

David Byrne couldn't have been less like rock's spectacular flameouts. He looked like a preppy kid. He had been an art student. His band, Talking Heads, made some of the smartest music in New York.

But four years after the first Talking Heads record, David was restless. In 1981, he collaborated with the influential and inventive producer and musician Brian Eno on *My Life in the Bush of Ghosts,* one of the first albums to "sample" recorded music made by others. When he met me, a few months later, he was open to another experiment—particularly with a choreographer whose early dances had a few things in common with his tense, angular onstage moves.

Not that he had seen my company. Not that I had really listened to his music. David and I just trusted Bill, so we plunged in and created *The Catherine Wheel*. The ideas David brought to our piece gave me much I could work with. His range was ambitious; he was among the first young Western musicians to investigate world music. And I had no problem that he wanted to write lyrics—which are often a burden in an evening of dance—because he was using words as sounds. Anything that could generate a new sound was catnip for him.

Before anyone else I worked with, David had a large interest in technology. He loved to tinker, adjust, experiment. He would happily bang on pans filled with water or pull a computer apart. A reporter once watched David and a digital-printing expert discuss—for an hour—the best technical approach to computerized reproduction of David's photos. Computer-monitor calibration, paper textures, the artistic possibilities of surveillance cameras: David stayed with the conversation, beat for beat. I've never met anyone with a bigger appetite for information.

Looking back, I see the rich variety of my musical collaborators. Bob Dylan was a poet; words came first for him, and in the early, folkie years of his career, it was key that those words have political and cultural bite. Elvis Costello, born thirteen years after Dylan, made music that was also lyric-driven, but so many of those lyrics were fused to such high-energy music that the songs came at you like a physical force. David Byrne, a contemporary of Costello's, found in music a way to merge fashion, community, technology, and a kind of urban good cheer. Billy Joel's great gift is his common touch—an ability to tell stories about the under-the-surface poetry in ordinary lives.

CHAPTER 5

Collaborating with an Institution

Institutions are massive. They have infrastructures. Traditions. And, above all else, an instinct for their own survival. Think: the Supreme Court, the army, the church, the New York Yankees. These seem vastly more overwhelming than, say, a small business or an artist.

Everybody knows this. And yet, when individuals collaborate with institutions, it too often happens that people fall into the very script they most want to avoid: David gets upset and reaches for his slingshot; Goliath straps on his boots. War commences.

Why does this happen?

As Seth Godin, a longtime observer of organizations, puts it: "Almost without exception, organizations are run by people who want to protect the old business, not develop the new one."

Unless their survival is at stake, institutions resist change and defend the status quo. Outsiders are free agents. With less to defend, they're prone to challenge things as they are.

We tend to romanticize the artist as a rebel. Think Michelangelo and the Vatican. Mozart and the church (and the monarchy). Van Gogh and the art establishment. Beethoven and just about everyone.

But think also of Bach, Haydn, Shakespeare, Rubens. They managed to get immense amounts of work done using huge institutions and their resources—and they accomplished this without being crushed by institutional stress. They may have lived in eras when it paid to be humble. But they were also very good politicians.

In 1999 a young LeBron James learned a version of this lesson when he joined the basketball squad at his new high school in Akron, Ohio. St. Vincent–St. Mary is a well-established institution with strict standards and rules, and James wasn't just the new kid, he was African-American in a mostly white private school. LeBron did not arrive at St. Vincent–St. Mary alone. He came with friends—a ready-made support system known as the Fab Four, that had a common passion: basketball. James didn't remain the new kid/outsider for long; he led the team to three state championships.

But he and his teammates became champions by belonging to the institution of St. Vincent–St. Mary, which has clear and absolute standards that apply to all its students. James is now professional basketball's marquee player. But once upon a time, the fifteen-year-old rising star and a strong institution met in the middle. And because the school's methods were sound and the boys shared its goals, good things followed.

If you can leave your personal baggage at the door, successful collaborations with institutions may be more available than you think.

I've had a long—more than thirty years—relationship with American Ballet Theatre. I've lived and worked through four administrations and three genera-tions of dancers. When I returned for the umpteenth time to make my sixteenth ballet for the company in 2008, I brought many lessons from the past along with the sure knowledge that things had changed since my last ABT ballet in 2000.

Maybe I knew too much.

ABT likes to promote its dancers. When I made my debut there, it was with Baryshnikov, a rising star who needed only a showcase for his immense talent. This time out, I've been given Ethan Stiefel and Herman Cornejo, two of its most accomplished principal dancers. My goal is clear.

But now I have worked so often at ABT that I also identify with the institution. That is, I think hard about its resources and how best to allocate them. I'm acutely aware of its vast budget and its constant fund-raising efforts. ABT wanted a big ballet to premiere on the stage of the Metropolitan Opera; in beginning to schedule rehearsals I was extremely conscious of the cost of rehearsal time for a full company. And I thought to minimize costs by creating a ballet in small units that could be pulled apart like Legos. This is done occasionally with sections in full-length ballets. But in this case I was building different layers separately that would ultimately be joined in the full scene.

This is a very unusual way to build a ballet; because it is to be performed in real time, it's best to build a ballet in real time. This one, called *Rabbit and Rogue*, was built schematically, as illustrated sequences on diagrams and computers.

Once again, as in Miami, I'd be working with dancers before I had the music. This time, I was more optimistic about a smooth path to a happy conclusion because writing scores is all that Danny Elfman does. Like Elvis Costello, he had once been a performer; he was the leader of a rock band called Oingo Boingo. But he'd transitioned to writing music that's recorded against a stopwatch.

Among his credits: the theme for *The Simpsons* and the soundtracks for *Mission: Impossible*, most of Tim Burton's movies (*Batman,* most notably), *Men in Black, Good Will Hunting,* and *Milk.*

Movie directors like their composers to give them a feeling for the score as early as possible so they have an idea of the soundtrack before going to the expense of recording. To provide directors with something that actually sounds like the score, Danny has mastered a complex, sophisticated music software called Digital Performer.

While this is extremely useful, what I value even more is Danny's outrageous energy and enthusiasm; if you needed a blood transfusion, you'd go to him first. He's a ferocious worker—at our first meeting he handed me a CD with ten tracks labeled, reasonably, "Ideas." His first question: "Is it movable?" I explained that thinking in the head is very different from thinking with the feet and I hadn't worked up to that yet.

I start to address Danny's "movable" question in the summer of 2007, when I'm in the studio with four ABT dancers who will be a part of the ensemble, ultimately to be cast as sixteen. In two weeks we create much of the chorus material. During this period, I also build a number of solo variations for Ethan. When I take a step back, I see that the dancing seems to fall into five different families of movement. And Danny and I begin to think of ways to develop some of the ten tracks I think are kinetic into five different sections.

In the fall, I begin the next rehearsal period. Now I have the second principal man, Herman Cornejo, for two hours a day. And I have time with two principal couples. I see some lovely dancing. I look forward to our next phase after the New Year.

All of this work I am, of course, documenting on video as a reference for when we begin to rehearse the ballet with all its component parts in one room. I spend a lot of time with this footage, considering its possibilities as any editor does with the day's rushes.

I begin to assemble the ballet parts in January. Danny is hitting his marks, attends a number of rehearsals, adjusts the score with a nip here and a tuck there. Soon I have a complete synthesizer version of the score. I feel we're getting close.

On video we look good. With one reservation: Getting the Legos to stack in real time is difficult because many dancers are out with injuries during this rehearsal period. Ultimately the rehearsal period ends with the ballet finished on my video edit but never seen in real time and space because the entire cast has yet to be in the room at the same time.

My Lego approach—turning a piece into modules that require only a few dancers—is prescient if you are making a virtual ballet. But this is a real ballet that will have a brush-up rehearsal period later in the spring, then premiere at the Met; the prospects are worrisome. Ultimately I can't believe what I can't see. And while I liked what I felt the ballet's possibilities were and loved the video, I was becoming concerned about its being birthed for live performance.

Concerned? More like worried. With holes in the first cast, no second casts, no covers, and an assistant double-scheduled, I can quit—I have that option. But as I've said, I've never used that clause, even when a principal I had come to the Paris Opera to make a ballet for bolted to join London's Royal Ballet just before I arrived.

Art, I remind myself, is the collaboration of fantasy and reality, and reality is either perfect except for the problems or, if I'm in an Oriental mood, perfect all the time. It's my vision against chaos. Why let chaos win?

As a choreographer, my task is to make the best possible work with the dancers I find in the room on any given day.

As a director—the person in charge—my task is to identify a champion who can deal with my problems and questions. That is, someone high on the organization chart and, ideally, the person who initiated this collaboration. No point burdening anyone of lesser stature.

At the Joffrey, my champion was the company's founder. But at ABT, it's hard to identify a champion. A much larger company, its structure and priorities are less clear.

ABT's wise heads nod sagely: "This is how it is. The dancers will get it together for the Met." I'm sure their track record supports this view. I'm unconvinced.

Kevin McKenzie, the company's artistic director, calls daily with updates on dancers' availability. David Lansky, now the company's general manager but a baby in stage management when I began in 1975, gets the old techies to make a run to the warehouse. And he personally lugs back huge linoleum rolls to put on the floor of a very large studio that ABT has recently acquired, one that begins to approach the mammoth proportions of the Met stage. Through it all, Norma Kamali calmly pins the ballerinas' costumes.

Before I start any collaboration, I list exactly what resources I'll require to do the job and then try to find out if the institution is prepared to provide them.

In life as in art, Rogue chases Rabbit. My biggest problem is getting the linchpins of the ballet, Rogue Ethan and Rabbit Herman, together. Apart they are fantastic. Ethan is knowledgeable, shrewd, driven, and inspired in his phrasing. Herman, eight years younger, is an amazing athlete with a double *revoltade* and a speed that is blistering at the beginning of the fourth movement, when he dances one of the world's longest distance sprints. Think of them together!

Many of the women are injured as well. With the cutbacks in the economy, the Met performance schedule remains the same—but the spring rehearsal period has been reduced. The company, ramping up to the season, must mount nine full-length ballets as well as the *Rabbit and Rogue* program. It is a huge load.

Danny has his problems, too. As he begins his rehearsals, he observes that transfer from Digital Performer to live musicians is always grueling, but this particular piece is an outright monster of coordination. Danny and I both know that we can't let these kinds of details pull us down, that we must protect the performers' spirits and their confidence for the performances.

Danny takes the long view and is hopeful that the orchestra will have mastered the score by the third performance. I'm less optimistic. I know the reality—there will be last-minute substitutions at every performance, and these musicians will never have rehearsed with the conductor. "Excellent" and "accurate" recede as goals. "Done is beautiful" is beginning to look good.

Neither of us speaks the obvious. Can it be that our sophisticated technological programs have outstripped the reality we can accomplish given our resources?

Maybe my January rehearsal composite video alongside Danny's Digital Performer track will be the best realization of *Rabbit and Rogue* we will ever see. Maybe virtual has won out on this one, making Danny and me the experienced dreamers chasing after reality the rabbit. In sum, perhaps this ballet best exists as what we thought was the draft—a work whose body is chasing its shadow.

Can it get worse? ABT opened its season with a gala premiere program at the Met. While *Rabbit and Rogue* will not premiere for three weeks, almost all the female principal dancers now are injured. And ABT's Met repertory performances mean I won't have rehearsal time for ten days. Never before have I not known who would be premiering a ballet, nor have I dropped rehearsals for this length of time on the eve of an opening.

I sleep badly, waiting for outright disaster. Our first stage dress rehearsal goes well enough, although the dancers—all of whom are performing in the evenings—must walk their steps and the orchestra is erratic.

And Paloma Herrera may not be able to perform. This is a grave disappointment for us both—for us all. I have a deep past with Paloma; I've created four ballets for her since she came to ABT seventeen years ago, and she is one of the main reasons I am making this ballet. Poor Kevin is calling in now three times a day from the Met with updates on dancers' injury status and role recasting.

Opening night for *Rabbit and Rogue* is the usual exchange of merde gifts—little cards and small flowers. Huge bouquets arrive from fans. Everyone is on eggshells.

Tonight I am trying a stoic approach: It will be what it will be. Keep breathing. Keep reminding yourself that what you want to see—what you have been looking at for almost a year now—is probably not what you are going to see tonight.

Curtain goes up: Ethan's onstage. Hallelujah. A spot cue misses him at one point, but the lighting crew should know its moves better second show. Ethan exits. Herman—that wondrous rabbit—dashes in behind, adorable, bouncy, faster than you can believe. Ethan reappears and the chase starts off. I want to cheer.

The quartet—not the one that is on the video, nor the one that had done much of the rehearsing in January, but a nonetheless spirited quartet—makes its first entry and its lead lieutenant holds them together.

And the ensemble: I count quickly. Yes: eight men and eight women. I know we have one second-cast female out there, because we had to pluck one first-cast woman for the quartet. And while this cast will be dancing full out together for the first time tonight, their experience in holding formations in countless other choreographers' ballets means that if they keep their wits about them they will be fine. And they do.

So it goes. Now it is about the ballerina in the third movement. And something wonderful happens—Paloma Herrera dances. When the curtain went up, I didn't know if she'd be the one onstage; I had rehearsed two other dancers, and I fully expected to see a brave but awkward performance by one of them. But there was Paloma.

Only those backstage and a few of us out front know how courageous this performance is—we are torn between wanting to applaud and holding our breath. But she's pulling it off, performing on grit and experience. She knows how to cheat her way around the impossible moves and how to emphasize the moments she can use to her advantage. She makes of it great drama, looking joyous, transported. But not injured.

In any collaboration, no one likes to let colleagues down. Crisis focuses energy. When it really matters, people rise to the occasion.

This kind of triumph is more familiar to us when it occurs, unscripted, in sports. If you're a baseball fan, you will recall the 1988 World Series between the Los Angeles Dodgers and the Oakland Athletics, when Dodgers star Kirk Gibson wasn't expected to play. He had a stomach virus. His legs were injured.

The night before the first game, he'd slept with his knees wrapped. In the morning, he couldn't walk without pain. At the stadium, he had an injection to dull the pain. Throughout the game, he was in the training room, being treated with ice on his knees. He told his wife to go home—no way could he play.

Then the opportunity arose: bottom of the ninth inning, his team one run down, a runner on base, two outs. He told himself, "I'll hear the fans, I won't feel the pain."

Gibson limped up to the plate. On the sixth pitch, Gibson didn't really swing the bat—it was more like he thrust it in the way of the ball. But he was strong.

And he connected. The ball sailed over the fence. And Gibson somehow gimped his way around the bases, a hero.

In the hallway afterward, I see Stiefel, Cornejo, Paloma—they're exhilarated. Gimpy. Tearful. High. The complicated feelings of great performers after a show. At moments like this, the choreographer becomes a shield, a shoulder, a shrink.

Then we're together: all the dancers, all the staff, many patrons, parents—not just the *R&R* cast but the whole company—onstage afterward for a toast Kevin and David have organized, for me, for the dancers, for ABT, for tradition. For getting it up. For us all doing our best, season after season, year after year.

I could be disappointed, but why? This has been my response many times in the past, and, with it, the impulse to blame others. Yes, the machine had been tested and it had its faults. But for better or worse, this particular machine is family. And in family, disappointments become lessons.

No company other than ABT had the resources, the dancers, or the will to commission a *Rabbit and Rogue*. Yes, according to the video many things went wrong. But things went wrong and the ballet still exists. Whether it goes into the bloodstream of dance, time will tell.

Or maybe it will be that ballet assembled on video promises another way for the future, presenting a virtual art constructed apart from the collaboration with reality that the physical world requires. Maybe I will come to interpret the title differently in the future. Maybe the machines will help the Rogue artist get closer to the perfection in his visions, those astonishing Rabbits of possibility so effortlessly flitting about in the artist's agile, rapid mind. Maybe our poor Rogue, older and wiser, and also slower, will no longer have to plod through reality to find a compromised bunny hunkered down and whimpering after his many miles of chase. Maybe.

If this collaboration with ABT was exhausting, it was mostly because it delivered a new and painful lesson in collaboration. Could everyone see the problems? Oh yes. And everyone knew the machine is heavy and slow to turn.

So the first lesson is patience. Change never occurs at the speed that outsiders crave; our metabolisms are tuned too high, our dreams are too urgent. By necessity, we are fast and nimble; by definition, institutions are slow and earthbound. And yet, in the process of these collaborations, change does come.

The other lesson is personal. I carried more baggage than I needed to— specifically, a knowledge of ABT's institutional priorities and resources that influenced my creative choices. I would have done better to forget my history there and relish being the guest.

It's easier when you're a first-time collaborator with an institution. Without history, you can see—and react to—what's in front of you. When you have history, you have ghosts.

If you're returning to an old collaboration, give yourself the option of beginning at the beginning. No end runs. No evocation of old problems and old solutions. Work gingerly to translate your hard-won lessons into the present. No stream is the same.

Noël Coward's advice for handling nagging conflicts and other troubles applies here: "Rise above it." Pretend nothing ever went wrong. He knew.

- Collaboration can be internal—an act of listening to others and then having a silent, private conversation with yourself.
- Price and audience are not compelling motivators. Your sense of quality is.
- Don't be afraid to fight your collaborator for what you know is true.

A sensible first impression of Norma Kamali is that she is strong, original, and a rule breaker, not that she is a great collaborator. And, indeed, her career has a definite "loner" quality.

When Kamali first thought of becoming a fashion designer, for example, she took a job as a reservationist with Northwest Airlines. A diversion? Not at all. Every weekend, she used her airline privileges to fly—for just $29—to London.

NORMA KAMALI

Fashion was joyously creative in the mid-1960s in London, and, every weekend, Kamali returned to New York with clothes for friends. Soon she realized that certain styles weren't being fully expressed. She couldn't sketch or sew, but she opened a shop—and added some clothes she had designed. Her clothes sold better than her London imports. And so, by a unique route, she became a designer.

Women responded to Kamali's clothes because they combined immense practicality with a strong and personal statement of style. More than forty years later, that combination is still at the core of Kamali's success. Along the way, she's taken no business partners or investors—a great achievement in itself.

How, then, does she collaborate?

Not in any way you can see—with Norma Kamali, collaboration is an internal process. She watches. She listens. She remembers. And then, when she designs, she factors in the desires of her client or customer.

This quiet, thoughtful way of working saves time and aggravation. It allows her to get it right the first time. And it frees her to do so many projects at once that, if you were unaware of her method, you might think she has legions of assistants hidden in a padlocked attic.

She's been a silent collaborator, with unusally varied influences, from the beginning, which may explain why, in addition to her innate creativity, her range is so vast. In the 1960s, she pioneered the vogue for hot pants. In the early 1970s, she was praised for swimsuits that emphasized the wearer's well-exercised thighs. In 1975, she made her first sleeping-bag coat. Later in the seventies, she designed the red swimsuit that Farrah Fawcett wore in the most popular poster of the decade. In 1981, she introduced stylish clothes made of sweatshirt-fleece fabric.

Kamali is also a shrewd trend watcher in fields far removed from fashion design. In the early 1980s, she decided it was wiser to make fashion videos than to present runway shows. In the 1990s, she was a fashion pioneer on the Internet. And in every decade, she reaches out in all directions. One day, she's teaching art and design in New York schools. Another day might find her designing costumes for one of my dances.

In our work together, I'm continually amazed by her attention to detail—and her pragmatism in dealing with people. She always manages to find a way of accommodating each dancer's proportions, while still welding the designs into a whole. Her costumes are timeless.

Of late, Kamali has forged a creative partnership with Walmart, the budget-conscious megastore. There her jersey wrap dress sells for $20, her twill pants for $15. At these prices, most designers couldn't protect the quality of their designs.

Kamali showed Walmart a way of manufacturing that brings the clothes in at the correct price points without compromising fit or quality. Indeed, she insisted on it. And Walmart, like so many others in the last four decades, understood that it was smarter to work with her than fight her.

The proof, as *The New York Times* reported, came when the NK line was unveiled at Walmart in Westbury, New York, and customers thronged the designer. When women asked her to sign their receipts, she cried.

CHAPTER 6

Collaborating with a Community

Back in the days of three television networks, a handful of film studios, and a dozen theaters near Times Square, we could talk about "audience" as if there were only one. Of course there was some fringe culture, but compared to mainstream media it wasn't much. All of America, it seemed, knew who had appeared on *Ed Sullivan* on Sunday and could speak knowledgeably about the Saturday night movie.

No more. Entertainment is now "on demand," and demand includes our choice of delivery system. That splintering of the audience has also shattered our concept of community—a virtual tribe of like-minded people who have never met one another is now as legitimate a definition of community as a religious congregation, a club, or a political party.

When I leave New York to choreograph an evening of dance, I like to give a lecture about the work I've made. It's not just a way for me to see what the local dance community is like and prepare its members for my pieces, it's a way for me to put my efforts into a single frame. More and more, I feel I need to do that—people get their information from multiple sources, and what they think they know can be poorly interpreted or just plain wrong.

There's another reason I like to talk, and that's to listen. The passive audience died when message boards became the rage on a young Internet. Now, with blogs and more, the audience is not just active, it's noisy. It seizes the microphone. It insists on being heard. And whether the commentary is wise or shrill, it is heard.

Fine with me. I like direct, unintermediated experience. I crave an audience that cares. And I welcome the opportunity to be accountable—to declare the worth of my offering and to defend it.

In September of 2008, following my collaborations in Miami and New York City, I went to Seattle to make two ballets for Pacific Northwest Ballet. I wanted to simplify this third collaboration of the year, so I chose music already written. Then, well before I boarded a plane, I sketched both ballets thoroughly. With so much of the creative work done in advance, I could turn my thoughts to extending my collaboration beyond the ballet audience; I wanted to find ways to relate to the larger community so more people might understand how it is that these two ballets actually do connect to their daily lives.

In Seattle, I'll be far more visible during the preparation of the program than I usually am. I'll clear hours for interviews. I'll go to cocktail parties and dinners for donors. I'll schedule open rehearsals so patrons of the ballet can watch me work with dancers. And, just before the premiere, I'll give a free lecture.

Why Seattle?

Two reasons.

First, because Seattle is a communications center—Microsoft began here, and the entrepreneurial spirit generated around that giant has inspired many more innovators to bring us fast, easy ways to communicate digitally. Costco and Starbucks are also headquartered here, and, like Microsoft, those companies and their employees are active in the ballet, the symphony, the museums. They give more than money; they attend rehearsals, serve on arts boards, attend dinners, ask questions. If any community can appreciate the idea of "art for the people," this is it.

Collaborating with the community might seem like an expensive "extra" in a time of shrinking budgets, but it's always struck me as a terrific investment. The more special your cause and your knowledge, the more important it is that you reach out to the community. There's plenty of money to sell soft drinks, only pennies to market dance. So what you do for free is the closest your cause comes to promotion. If you've got nothing to hide, throw open the doors!

Collaborating with the community is not entirely selfless. Still, it's a long shot that it will produce a massive influx of newly interested people. More realistically, it's like tithing—only instead of money, you're giving a percentage of your creative energy. And like a lot of charity, you don't know whom you're helping or how. Your aim is to introduce and explain what you do. In a sense, you're throwing seeds randomly, hoping they'll sprout.

My second reason for making this commitment in Seattle is that Peter Boal, artistic director of Pacific Northwest Ballet, has a keen sense of community. Though he has a company to run and a family at home, he seems to go anywhere when a Seattle cause asks. And his dancers are also giving of themselves, demonstrating their art in public schools, staging special rehearsals for the community free of charge, and funding ballet classes for inner-city kids. PNB is a model of a community-conscious arts institution.

Peter is an ideal partner for me in another way: While I'm surely not like a mother to him, he's very much like a son to me. At eighteen, he became a company member of the New York City Ballet. Soon after he joined, George Balanchine passed away. Peter's first appearance in a new ballet was a piece that Jerome Robbins and I made in Balanchine's honor.

And there's one more connection. Peter started teaching at the NYCB even before he'd reached his peak as a dancer, a clear sign that he saw goals larger than his own career. Because I consider choreography and teaching as pretty much the same thing, I've admired Peter for decades. So it was in a multiple identity as fellow dancer, choreographer, and teacher that I came to Seattle.

What I see in Peter's company is a very civilized environment. But it's not just a veneer of good manners. He respects the people he works with, and that makes it easier for them to respect him right back. And he deals directly and in the moment. Like a pastor with his congregation, Peter begins classes with a brief word to his dancers on behavior. In the class I attended, one dancer had missed a rehearsal without calling in. Peter addressed the matter before pliés. No reason to stew or ruminate; deal with it, and move on.

We hear a lot about motivation, and how great coaches bring out great desire to succeed in their students. I have never found that to be true, and I think the greatest coaches tend to say success is self-motivated. Former Harvard rowing coach Harry Parker—who with fourteen undefeated seasons may be the most successful sports coach of the last half century—believes that the will to excel exists within each athlete and is not something that a coach can, or should, attempt to instill. His crews agree. "In life as in sport, you don't do it for the Gipper, or for Seiji Ozawa, or for Harry," says a Parker veteran. "Harry opens a space into which an athlete can pour his passion. There's no room for it when the coach is in the spotlight."

As I ask the dancers to become close to the material, I work to get closer to them. Because I'm new here, I must watch hard and speak last. This is, at bottom, just good manners. There are names to learn, quirks to note, customs to observe. Until I know the names of twenty-five dancers, I really don't have the right to say very much of substance to them. (Did I say twenty-five? This is a year that has had me working with three different companies; that means learning my way around more than one hundred dancers.)

Names learned, I get down to cases. Some dancers are stronger than others; some have technique to burn. And some have interesting quirks: the ability to leap high, or turn easily—but only to the right. Soon I see who can give me what I need, who loves to dance, who dances for the paycheck, who should not be in the front line. Outside the dance world, this individual attention is not understood—or noticed. You see a company of dancers performing in sync. What you don't see is that the choreographer doesn't train a company, but rather twenty-five individuals. Out of many collaborations comes one.

This assessment requires a cold eye. Dancers accept a leader's assessment more readily if the leader is, like Peter, a player-coach. That's why it matters that, in his early forties, Peter can still demonstrate what he wants when he teaches. And that's one reason I train so religiously. Jerome Robbins told me that when he became too old to dance, he lost much of his ability to create dances. I'm not sure about that—Jerry, on a chair, was still a great choreographer—but I do think it bothered him greatly not to be able to show dancers what he wanted.

In *We Were Soldiers Once . . . and Young,* Lt. Gen. Harold Moore and Joseph Galloway remind us that, in the American Civil War, you rarely saw a good officer on horseback. Like his soldiers, he walked. How else could he know how they felt—and how battle-ready they were? As with so many things, the best view is the one that's close up.

Another large collaborative decision I made before coming to Seattle was to work as much as possible with PNB's in-house resources. Though it's more comfortable for me to work with a team I know well, I can't ignore the fact that Seattle has built a quality orchestra, and that PNB's scenic and wardrobe shops are among the best in the world of the ballet.

Beyond the excellence of the Seattle team lies another reason to work in-house. Bringing in outsiders can upset a company's equilibrium and generate paranoia. Outsiders are an explicit judgment: The in-house staff is inadequate. Sometimes it's true.

More often, though, choreographers bring in their own designers because they want as much security and efficiency in their own lives as possible. As I'm overlapping so many projects in one year, the more consistent the team, the easier my life will be. But what's the priority—my comfort, or the enthusiasm of the company and its community?

I think of my friend Milos Forman. Like any smart film director, he believes in surrounding himself with the most talented people he can find. And then, if the relationship is good, he works with them again and again.

Forman met Miroslav Ondricek at Czechoslovakia's Barrandov Studios in the early 1960s. Ondricek was learning to shoot feature films, and in 1963, Forman had one for him to shoot.

Ondricek would go on to work for some of the world's most admired directors, but he always returned to collaborate with Forman. In quick succession, they made *Hair, Ragtime,* and *Amadeus*—and Ondricek was nominated for Academy Awards for both *Ragtime* and *Amadeus*.

Ondricek and Forman are a great creative fit. And surely there is also the advantage of sharing references from decades earlier—and of communicating with nothing more than a gesture. Or a word in a language that no one else on the set can speak.

Usually when I am working on a ballet, I go stony faced by the receptionist to change my clothes and get into the studio before a stray thought can intrude on the day's dancing. In Seattle, however, because I have done so much advance work, I can afford the time to walk the hallways and make the rounds first thing in the morning. The facility here is very well designed, and I can check in with scenics, wardrobe, therapy, publicity, fund-raising, Peter and his right-hand man, Doug, and the rehearsal assistants—all before going into the studio to work.

I find it very reassuring and grounding that everyone is so excited about working together on the ballets. And when Peter asks me to talk to the staff shortly after I've arrived, I'm happy to do it not just because the company is welcoming, but because it gives me a chance to practice the lecture that will be my principal gift to the community.

This lecture is a kind of probe, a reaching out to strangers in the hope that we're connected in one specific way—a longing for meaning. In a fragmented world, we want our lives to matter. And one important way we judge that is by our work. If you are a carpenter, a teacher, a nurse, or a coach, you have a good idea at the end of each day what you achieved. You built a wall, showed kids how to do long division, eased the pain of the sick, helped your players win. If you are in the arts, it's much more difficult to measure your accomplishments.

Recognizing and acknowledging quality is one factor here. Connection with others is just as important. Once upon a time, there was no difference between a bricklayer and a composer. All work was an offering to the deity, and thus, all work had equal meaning. But in the twentieth century that changed and art came to exist for its own sake.

The change is sometimes called modernism. But let's not get bogged down in language. The issue is meaning—or rather, the lack of it. The idea here is that human life no longer has spiritual meaning. We are not part of a loving society but rather are all in an ego-driven "army of one," each the center of an absurd cosmos, taking such happiness as we can find. Collaboration? Why bother? You only live once; grab whatever you can.

In 1897, Leo Tolstoy anticipated all this in a book called *What Is Art?* As a Christian and a moralist, he distinguishes between "good" and "bad" art. In essence, he argues that "bad" art makes us feel alone; "good" art promotes feelings of brotherhood. It will surprise no one who has read any of Tolstoy that good art tends to feature honest labor, peasants toiling in the fields, folk songs and dances. His aristocratic Levin discovering the virtues of work alongside the laborers in *Anna Karenina* is one of my favorite descriptions of dance: the beauty of mowing, its efficiency and economy, the job done by the community in ranks, the grateful fatigue of the workers.

I was thinking about Tolstoy's praise for simple, universal, and uplifting art before I went to Seattle.

It's my feeling that we're at a crisis point, a moment of deciding what will happen to life on this planet. Is it meaningless and pointless, or have we— slowly and painfully—learned something about living creatively and in harmony with others? In short, will we take what we know about collaboration and act on it?

If my way of thinking and acting prevails, art becomes as central to life as— oh, entertainment. And then we'll come to see that art *is* entertainment, and that learning, improving ourselves, coming closer to our best selves is more rewarding than mindless "fun."

I'd like to share the themes of that Seattle lecture here. As you read, you may note that I don't cater to the audience or shrink from sharing what I've learned. Indeed, the more challenging the material, the more important it is *not* to dumb it down.

Trust the community to play its own role in the collaboration: to watch, enjoy, learn, judge.

Put your knowledge and point of view out there and hope the audience connects with it and becomes your collaborator, much as Coach K's pregame talks with Duke's basketball spectators convert them into the team's "sixth man."

Like this . . .

Every successful dance performance gives the sense of a closed system—that whatever carefully selected events transpire onstage when the curtain goes up will have played themselves out when the curtain comes down, and that there is a logic and a purpose for the dancers onstage that will be fulfilled during the course of the action. There can be no accounting for all this during the performance and there will be no footnotes after the show. What you see is what you get.

During a lecture, I'm not there to tell you what you'll see. Rather, the lecture is about how I got to the ideas that underpin what you'll see. What I was reading while I was creating. What I was thinking about myself and our lives together. It is this adventure—Where did these events come from? What do they mean?—that I can share with a lecture audience.

All this motivating content—as I say, never visible in performance until discussed but, once explained, never to be missed again—is a way of developing a life for the dances that is different from what the performances can accomplish and often helps an audience find meaning where before was mystery.

The point of the two new Seattle dances is to show them back-to-back; they are a collaboration within a collaboration. First a string quintet by Johannes Brahms, Opus 111, then a work for string orchestra by Vladimir Martynov, *Autumn Ball of the Elves*. These two pieces, written almost exactly one hundred years apart, present a comparison that directly abuts late Romantic lushness to postminimalist aridness.

I begin the lecture with the Brahms. I show slides of the reams of notes and the marked score I brought to Seattle. Then, without music, the dancers share some of the phrases that become the ballet's geometry, showing parallels between the dance and the architecture of the music.

Next the Martynov. I show the simple units that I gave the dancers as class exercises, first performing them "straight" and then morphing the units into an elaborate collage of themselves. This could be done in silence, but I choose to play Terry Riley's *In C* as accompaniment. This music, first performed in 1964, is often credited as the beginning of minimalism in music—Steve Reich was in the original *In C* band, and Reich's music has had a large impact on Martynov.

As we dance, the set director oversees the building of our high wall of a set. While the dancers continue their constructions, combining, recombining, and re-recombining, I talk about how this set—a barren corner where three of our *Afternoon Ball* dancers, a bit like street runaways in Seattle, will find a home— represents an aesthetic and existential dilemma, a metaphor for how artists have come to box themselves in, the walls closing bit by bit as the options left to twentieth-century art are reduced.

Since the early twentieth century, modernists, postmodernists, atonalists, serialists, and minimalists have challenged the lushness and complexities of late-nineteenth-century music—masterworks such as Opus 111. The twentieth century became reactionary as the avant-garde jettisoned the work of previous generations, and, rather than evolve through it, chose instead to replace it from the ground up.

Martynov, as a second-generation minimalist, sees the only logical extension of less and less to be nothing, so the chaste and sterile beauty he slowly builds in the beginning spins inevitably toward nihilism, whirling ever faster and spiraling ever closer to the exact center of its vortex, finally imploding like the Manhattan Project's "Fat Man" about two-thirds of the way through the score.

You can only deconstruct so far. What is there after the particles in an atom? What way out of this dead end, this throwing out of the Romantic baby with the minimalist bathwater? Where do we go from here? Where's the escape from the corner?

What Martynov does next is shocking. He introduces a melody. A simple theme is, of course, a basic no-no in twentieth-century music. Nonetheless, here is a very simple and very beautiful melody rising through all the dust and rubble as the composer doubles back to a universe where melody and grace once more hold sway. This suggests a nineteenth-century bourgeois world where one of our street kids finds refuge. The cold exterior corner becomes a warm and sheltering interior where an elegant couple performs its endless variations on the waltz.

Next Martynov begins to erase his nineteenth-century melody bit by bit, over-powering it with the repetitive sound of the minimalistic beginning of the piece. The work ends almost as it began, different only in that now the genial waltzing woman we saw in the warm interior corner comes to visit this modern place. As the minimalistic music becomes paler and paler, falling away until everything we have been hearing over and over begins to disappear along with the cool fading light, one of our street kids is left alone shivering. Finally, just before this light goes out, the graceful nineteenth-century lady wraps her arms about our last street survivor and a warmer light—one that we have never seen before in the ballet—begins to glow far in the distance.

Curtain.

The more you ask, the more you get back. The more you challenge an audience, the more challenging you can be to yourself.

I got something unexpected from this talk. Coming to Seattle with all my charts, graphs, and schemes, it was not until I wrote this lecture that I realized the simple fable at the heart of the story I was telling. As a child, my very favorite fairy tale was "The Little Match Girl," as read to me by my mother's mother. I'm sure I connected with the character of the hero as a girl. I'm sure I responded to her selfless devotion. But even more I'm sure I liked the message that in the end the child would not be left alone.

No audience will "see" the Match Girl association right off, though some might "feel" the reassuring effect of the ending. As a choreographer, I know dance must show its entire world in its performance. Yet I hope that by diving into the creation of the work I am helping the audience to realize certain cultural conclusions that are, I think, relevant to all our lives.

I conclude the lecture with Tolstoy.

Tolstoy was a contemporary of Brahms. And Tolstoy loathed the late Romantic sophistication evolved specifically by Brahms and Beethoven. But Tolstoy sold Brahms short. He missed that Brahms, too, had keened to simpler music, borrowing often from folk music for songs and melodies. Indeed, it was the robust music at the end of Opus 111 that inspired me to conclude the ballet in foot-stomping, rollicking unison. Brahms, too, knew his peasants.

With a little guidance, I feel the audience can see that my dancers and the Martynov reinforce this same message. Modernists have sold the Romantics short. Dead-ended, we need to go back for another look. This is what Martynov is saying. And this is why the Brahms and the Martynov are programmed together—they complement each other. Between them they give hope to us all in the form of a future imported from our past.

Am I asking a great deal of my audience? You bet. But I've found that the more you share all your intentions, inform all of your collaborators—your audience as well as your performers—and trust them to use their imaginations, the more they will learn and grow. And the more respect you will find in the community.

- An audience has a greater tolerance for originality than is often believed.
- Letting an audience in on the joke creates a community of collaborators.

His father wanted to be an actor, so he moved his wife and two children from Texas to Hollywood. When he didn't make it, he became withdrawn and sullen. The boy's "attitude" enraged him, and, once, he beat his son quite seriously. "I tell you this story of my father and me," Steve Martin has written, "to let you know I am qualified to be a comedian."

In addition to an unhappy childhood, Steve Martin had a geographical asset—he lived two miles from Disneyland. He got a job there when he was ten, watched enough magic to perform, and was soon demonstrating

STEVE MARTIN

tricks eight to twelve hours a day. By fifteen, he was doing magic acts for Cub Scouts. By twenty, he was performing in comedy clubs.

"The opportunity to perform four and five times a day gave me confidence and poise," Martin has recalled. That endless stream of audiences also provided feedback and guidance. "They love it when the tricks don't work," he's said. "I started to think that the future of a serious magician was limited."

Martin was also studying philosophy in college, and it had a powerful effect. "It changed what I believe and what I think about everything," he writes in his memoir. "Something about non sequiturs appealed to me. In philosophy, I started studying logic, and they were talking about cause and effect, and you start to realize, 'Hey, there *is* no cause and effect! There is no logic!

There is no anything!"'That led him to ask questions that don't ordinarily occur to comedians: "What if there were no punch lines? What if there
were no indicators? What if I created tension and never released it?"

Once the punch line became his enemy, Martin was liberated. Like a
magician who shows audiences how he does his tricks, he took audiences inside his routines and made them his collaborators—a community
of people laughing at what was far from traditional comedy. He wore a
white-vested suit so he'd look "like a visitor from the straight world who
had gone seriously awry." He'd twist balloons, play his banjo, don nose
glasses. At the end of a show, he might lead the audience out of the club,
guiding them into McDonald's or another club.

One night, at the end of a show at a college, Martin realized there was
no stage exit, so as he walked out through the audience, he ad-libbed. The
students followed him onto the campus, all the way to a drained swim-
ming pool. "Everybody into the pool!" Martin shouted, "and they did." He
said he was going to "swim" on top of them, and they got it—they passed
him hand over hand as he pretended to do the crawl. "That night," he has
recalled, "I went to bed feeling I had entered new comic territory."

Backstage in Vegas, Elvis Presley gave him a spot-on review: "Son, you have an
ob-leek sense of humor." Martin pressed on. And, suddenly, he hit. An act that
once couldn't fill clubs was now selling out stadiums. *Saturday Night Live* and
movies were his for the asking. Steve Martin was America's "wild and crazy" guy.

For Martin, that massive acceptance was gratifying. But for him, it was
also a signal that it was time to move on—once everyone was in on the
joke, it wasn't really funny anymore.

CHAPTER 7

Collaborating with Friends

Intimacy married to creativity—it's hard to resist, this idea of working with people you know and like. Especially when you're having dinner with friends. There you are, everyone relaxed, and the conversation shifts to How It Might Be if you could only spend your days doing something worthy with people who share your ideas/politics/religion/values.

That enterprise would be frictionless, wouldn't it? No office politics, no double-dealing, just a solid team effort toward a shared goal. And in no time at all, you'd be rich/successful/fulfilled.

Not so fast. Let's consider the possibility that, at some point, you will have to say "no" to your friend and colleague. For you, that's a value-free "no," a "no" on the merits. But to your friend, does that "no" deliver more messages than you intended? Does that "no" wound? Is it too personal? Down the line, if you have Thanksgiving dinner with this colleague, will that "no" still be echoing over the turkey?

Reverse the scenario. Your collaborator tells you "no." Just business? Or does the rejection sting?

And how long do you want this collaboration with friends to last? A short-term commitment—"Let's put on a play!"—is one thing. An incorporated business is quite another. The first is a romp, an adventure; the second is a marriage, or, worse, a jail sentence.

A good collaborator is easier to find than a good friend. But in the hierarchy of values, I find it hard to top a real friend. If you've got a true friendship, you want to protect that. To work together is to risk it.

In my experience, it often happens that I make friends during a collaboration. On occasion, I have worked with friends. But always with great care.

It's been said of film that it records "death at work." Over two decades, Richard Avedon photographed my dances twenty-seven times, and I never once felt a dark shadow in the enterprise.

Dick was the first photographer who ever did more than take quick snapshots of me, and he spoiled me for anyone else. He was wildly prepared, in total control, up for any preplanned adventure. In the studio, he was intense. He had limitless energy and he threw that into a photo session—there was no downtime when you were working with him.

Dance photography is particularly difficult. You can get a great shot of the dancer's costume, position, and face—and miss the spirit completely. Dick never made that mistake, for the simple reason that he didn't photograph dance, he photographed movement. Let others take historically accurate pictures. Dick went for the drama. Which does not just "happen"—the "spontaneity" the viewer often sees in his photographs was carefully crafted. And crafted collaboratively. Before each session, we met at least once to discuss our purpose and the pictures that would fulfill it. Sometimes we drew. Sometimes we took Polaroids. The image we created was less important than the process—learning to speak a common language, struggling to see the same possibilities.

In this process, I found myself far outside the parameters of my own art. Nothing's more liberating than gaining a new perspective from a totally unlikely and "different" place. I like to think that happened for Dick, too, and that he also got a creative jolt from our sessions.

All artists have "signatures." Most guard them closely. Again and again, I've found that really smart and talented people don't hoard the "secrets" of their success—they share them. It isn't as if you could use their methods and duplicate their results. Excellence is about so much more than craft.

Dick was generous about sharing technical knowledge that I could take with me. He'd show me how to raise my chin just so . . . tilt it like this . . . now lower it a fraction. He taught me how to look into the lens, but not directly. He made me aware of the relationship between my cheekbones and the key light. And he created a collaboration between my eye and his camera. Just as he pressed the shutter, I'd squint ever so slightly; that would freeze my retina for an instant while the lens was open. In this way I could "see" the picture before it was processed.

Dick's technical mastery paled beside his vitality, made of equal parts energy and charm and speed. He had flair and audacity and all the oversize, expansive values. But it was the comfort zone he created that made the difference for me. Dick had researched and prepared; he'd talked through his ideas with me and heard mine. In the process, his studio became mine. Though he was very much in charge, it always felt as if we were cocreating.

The last time we worked together, Dick's assistant took a photograph of us together, hugging, touching. Then we took turns behind the camera. Dick got his shot, I got my shot.

Few might notice, but to me, the difference between these last two photos is huge. The one done by the assistant allowed us to touch. The individual shots we took of each other and then pasted together show two permanently separate people in the same frame, apart but willing to commit to each other. The first picture shows friends, the second a collaboration.

Richard Avedon taught me what Keats called "negative capability"—a willingness to suspend judgment and see reality as another might. That's creativity at its most openhearted. Those pictures of the two of us remind me that the ultimate best result of any collaboration is learning to look through your collaborator's eye.

When my friend Milos Forman asked me to choreograph his film version of the off-Broadway rock musical *Hair*, he was probably the most sought-after director in the world—his last film had been *One Flew Over the Cuckoo's Nest*, which won five Academy Awards, including one for best direction.

It was my impression that you can't collaborate with a film director. He's a king. Nothing happens until he gives the signal, and no film is developed if he doesn't think it should be. He has "final cut"—and every cut along the way. The best I thought I could hope for from Forman was a chance to make a small creative contribution that might bear a trace of my style.

Milos knew I had directed a television special about dance, that I wanted to do more, and that I could benefit from watching him. He didn't need for me to say a word for him to know that part of me wanted the camera on me, wanted to perform. He was, that year, the personification of opportunity.

Our first meeting was memorable because it was so obviously not like any meeting he'd ever had. Here he was, offering me a job; here I was, asking him to audition. I grilled him about his films, and how he made them, and how he saw *Hair,* and, not least, how he, as an Eastern European man, thought he could collaborate with an American woman.

And I asked something unprecedented from him—that he show me his films. Actually a difficult task, because in the 1970s, there were no DVDs. And videotapes weren't ubiquitous. A private showing of a movie meant the rental of a screening room, the hiring of a projectionist, to say nothing of tracking down a print. In this case, all for an audience of one.

To his credit, Milos didn't laugh at my request. He did show me his films, and talk about his choices, and listen to my suggestions. And that made me comfortable enough to sign on for what turned out to be a two-year commitment.

A film in production may be the ultimate experience in collaboration. It's like a military operation or a religious crusade. Hundreds of people are gathered together, often isolated in some remote location, all with a single purpose. It's long hours and in-jokes, secret alliances and public conflicts. It's people doing something better than you ever dreamed could be, done twenty times in a row.

And it's selfless, because you can see, going in, that most of what any one person does on a film doesn't make it into the movie. That didn't bother me. What I learned on that set was much more than I could say at the time.

From Milos Forman, I learned that collaboration depends on very precise communication—speaking to the right person at the right time in the right way.

- I learned that the way to speak to people—to speak to them so they're motivated to take their effort up a notch—is almost never to yell at them. Yelling is overkill.

- I learned that if you feel you're about to yell, retreat. When he felt anger rising, Milos would go to his trailer and sleep it off. My antidote for a pounding pulse was to hit the exercise room.

• I learned that you should have no scruples about getting what you absolutely need, to be endlessly resourceful, to go around, through, over, or under. Once a greatly revered actress loved the color of her dress, but Milos didn't like it at all. Rather than tell her to change the dress, he had the dress gradually tinted to the color he wanted.

• I learned how to be intimate in front of a hundred people as I watched Milos take an arm or hand, pet, poke, and stroke—communicating by touch almost as you would with an animal. Actors are desperate for attention; if you just rub their elbow ever so gently, if you suggest, Yes, I'm here with you, you've turned a nervous wreck into a believer. A cheap trick? Hey, it works. And not just on actors. There's a powerful truth in a human gesture: You are reaching out.

• I learned to accept suggestions and ideas gratefully from any and all. Milos welcomed everyone's suggestions, if they were for the good of "the baby," as he referred to the movie in process.

• I learned the power of "thank you." At every opportunity, dozens of times a day—you just can't say "thank you" too often.

And, finally, I saw Milos roll with the punches time after time, never losing sight of his goal, never compromising how he saw *Hair*, no matter what went "wrong."

Milos Forman and Richard Avedon became my friends during the course of a collaboration. Only once have I begun a collaboration with someone who was already one of my closest friends.

When I was just three years old, Jerome Robbins choreographed *Fancy Free,* and from then on he was famous. When I came to New York in the 1960s, I seemed to have no shyness about pushing myself into the classes of great choreographers. But meeting *Jerome Robbins?*

Finally, in 1974, I called him up and bluntly said it was silly that we didn't know each other. Over dinner, we became friends. I saw his work, he saw mine; we talked about dance incessantly. We listened to music. He loved scores, and we looked at them. But no collaborative idea emerged.

Then, a few years into our friendship, Jerry suggested we make a ballet together. I said no. And I held that position for years. He understood why: I valued his friendship much more than any jointly produced ballet and worried that the latter would cost the former.

Two choreographers, one dance. How would that work? Who'd win the nearly inevitable tug-of-war over resources and ownership? Jerry said that if we split everything equally, nothing could go wrong between us.

I kept thinking: "What is it they say about two cooks in the kitchen?" But it seemed silly to use folk wisdom in a conversation with one of the planet's most sophisticated theatrical minds.

I did ask: Might our ballet be narrative?

It might, Jerry said, if I had a story. Did I?

I didn't. But, ever the optimist, I said I was sure that we could make one up.

Jerry knew that stories are not made up. Better, he suggested that we do an abstract ballet.

Then I suggested Brahms's *Variations and Fugue on a Theme by Handel*—which was, I said, already a collaboration of sorts.

Jerry went to George Balanchine for his blessing and Balanchine agreed, provided we were talking about the orchestrated version. (Brahms originally wrote the work for two pianos.) There were, Balanchine said, more than enough "piano ballets" in the repertory.

So, here I was in a collaboration with a dear friend—without really knowing what we'd do together or how it would work.

Then Balanchine died. A world without Balanchine? His death made a huge void in the dance world—and in Jerry's life. And that created an urgency: Jerry wanted the Brahms/Handel to be the first piece to bear his name in the post-Balanchine era of the New York City Ballet.

Our first day of rehearsal at the NYCB was both exhilarating and excruciatingly sad. In the weeks after Balanchine's death, the entire company was in a suspended state of disbelief. Numb. Frozen. Here was young Peter Boal, who had just graduated from the school and was ready at last to have the master take his ten years of devotion in the studio to the next level—center stage. And here were the great ballerinas Merrill Ashley and Maria Calegari, honed to a precise edge by Balanchine's daily classes, now untethered.

It felt like sacrilege for me to suggest anything to these wonderful creatures, so lovingly and amazingly developed by the efforts and genius of Balanchine. He could have asked for anything and they would have performed; I wondered if I could ask enough. Jerry felt the same. We worried, but we had no choice. We were committed.

Very quickly, we came to the obvious: Our dance would be our offering—our memorial—to Balanchine. The dancers seemed to feel the same way. You could see it in their determination and fortitude. No matter how often I asked for a phrase or a lift to be repeated, they gave their best possible effort—they would have collapsed before giving less.

Even more impressive was the unspoken demand for innovation. It came from everywhere and everyone, from the assistants to the accompanists to the dancers. The New York City Ballet was humming with the desire—no, the absolute need—to try something new. That was what Balanchine had trained them to do; that is what dancing in historic repertory every night showed was the way.

I always want the new. But for this dance, I also wanted to reference Balanchine, utilizing his ballets as tribute. Though I didn't have a thorough knowledge of his ballets, I had an image of some of his great moments in mind, and in my own clumsy way I started assembling them. Jerry was strong with partnering, so I utilized that talent as well. Combining these elements, I began to generate variations on a theme—which, out of deference, was created by Jerry, who modeled it after Balanchine.

Jerry and I had begun with no rules, but had agreed to the concept of a game. It was very *West Side Story*—two teams, the Blues and the Greens. How did we choose colors? Jerry wanted blue, so I got green.

This was not just politeness or deference. It was also a dash of Eastern thinking—it is better for your survival if you bend in a strong wind. I'm no martial arts buff, but I've read and seen enough to know that one way to play is to use the energy of the opponent for your own ends. Here, there was no winning or losing, there was only the game. Jerry and I definitely enjoyed playing it.

We'd need two teams of dancers? Fine. Jerry took Merrill, I got Maria. But we kept changing, changing. Because that was Jerry. He liked to nudge, to fiddle; he was slow to commit, sit still, move on. I had watched this internal dance of his for many years, and I knew the next phase would be intense guilt and insecurity. He knew what he was doing, but he didn't believe he knew. He'd feel lost. My method was just do the work until it looked serviceable, then move on while I still sort of knew what I was trying to do. Later, when I could look at the whole piece, I might revisit it—no, *I would* revisit it, but still trusting my first instincts and trying not to fix what wasn't broken.

Two choreographers working together with such different temperaments need to stay out of each other's way. Jerry passed through my studio daily, and he always noticed that by the evening I usually had finished most of a variation begun early in the day. As our agreement was that we would bounce variations back and forth as in a badminton game, he liked to swap casts. "You take three of my women, I'll take two of your men," he'd say amiably, then he'd go off with the dancers and alter something in a variation, which meant I had to revisit it again the next day. Soon we were in full bog-down mode, repeatedly altering and revisiting each other's work.

At this point, Jerry suggested that we hold the premiere over to the next season. It fell to Lincoln Kirstein, cofounder of the NYCB, to weigh in. Which he did, loudly. "George would never have done that," he shouted at Jerry. "Get it up!"

I saw a way out: We'd just alternate variations. And that enabled us to finish the dance.

From the start, Jerry and I had pledged not to say who'd done what so the collaboration would feel more complete. On opening night of *Brahms/Handel,* what I saw on the stage of the State Theater were dancers performing new hybrids of movement. I felt proud and fulfilled. I think Jerry did too.

As for the ownership quotient—who did what?—that didn't really count for much. Sitting in the audience, I remembered an old wooden panel Jerry had given me that he had picked up somewhere in Europe from, he liked to say, a Gypsy wagon. It has two nearly identical dancing girls painted on it, one the reverse image of the other, one wearing blue and red, the other red and blue. Watching the dancers onstage, I could see what he had done and what I had done, and sometimes I knew I was watching his work and mine, two totally different approaches to the same music, simultaneously. Other times I genuinely could not tell where he'd left off and I'd begun.

And then Jerry, too, was gone, and with him, a conversation and friendship like no other. I'm grateful to have known him in this way and to be able to report that our friendship held up to the very end.

One recent summer, *Brahms/Handel* was performed again. It seemed not at all strange, as I came out of the theater after the performance, that I walked into sunshine with rain pouring through it. Dance is the ephemeral art; it literally disappears. How ironic that *Brahms/Handel* seemed a way of keeping Jerry with me forever and also of sharing us both with generations of young dancers.

• Just being with Robbins, I learned how to look for the obvious, never to forget common sense and to use it with flair.

• Working with Jerry, I learned that boundaries need to be clear. I encouraged him, and vice versa, but I never said, "Jerry, I've got a problem," or asked, "What did you just do?"

• I kept in reserve the knowledge that I could always get Jerry to laugh. Sometimes it's humor that allows you to be really serious.

• Most important, I learned with Robbins that there is no ownership in a successful collaboration.

So on the question of collaborating with a friend, I generally don't recommend it. But I'm glad I've done it. I don't begrudge the extra energy and care it took to make sure the friendships survived the collaborations.

- It is possible for collaborators to have a total personal/professional relationship.
- In some kinds of partnerships—science and technology, especially—two can move faster than one.
- In some fields, at some times, a woman can advance more rapidly if her partner is male.

Maria Skodowska's parents were teachers who lost most of their money in ill-fated patriotic schemes in their native Poland. But their daughter was brilliant. And dedicated—in order to study in Paris, she lived in a room so cold she had to pile all her clothes over her to stay warm on winter nights. Soon she had a degree in mathematics from the Sorbonne.

MARIE AND PIERRE CURIE

In Paris in 1894, she met Pierre Curie, who taught physics and chemistry. They were uniquely suited by their common interests and iconoclastic outlook; their bond was total. As Pierre wrote to her, "It would be a fine thing . . . to pass our lives near to each other, hypnotized by our dreams: your patriotic dream, our humanitarian dream, and our scientific dream." The next year, when they married, they used the money they received to buy two bicycles. That was their relaxation. The rest of the time, they worked together in the lab—that is, in a primitive, shedlike structure that had been a storeroom and machine shop.

They were never happier than when they were working, for their union allowed them to move very quickly from discovery to discovery. In 1897, when Marie had a child, she saw that going home to breast-feed took too much time, so she found a wet nurse, turned child care over to her father, and rededicated herself to the lab.

The Curies discovered radioactivity—a word they coined—and, in 1903, won (along with Henri Becquerel) the Nobel Prize in Physics. What had not yet been discovered: Radioactivity is deadly. They left radioactive materials out in the lab, carried them in their pockets, watched them glow in the dark. As a result, they contracted radiation poisoning—a century later, some of their notebooks still are stored in heavy lead boxes.

Pierre died in 1906. Marie put a picture of herself in his coffin, "the picture of her who had the happiness of pleasing you enough so that you did not hesitate to offer to share your life with her, even when you had seen her only a few times. You often told me that this was the only occasion in your life when you acted without hesitation, with the absolute conviction that you were doing well. My Pierre, I think you were not wrong. We were made to live together, and our union had to be."

In 1911, Marie Curie won the Nobel Prize in Chemistry; she is one of only two scientists to win the Nobel in a second field. But honors to women did not extend far in those days. She was denied membership in the all-male French Academy of Sciences. And when she had a romance with a scientist who had left his family, the scandal was all about her.

When she died in 1934, Albert Einstein commented that Marie was "of all celebrated beings, the only one whom fame has not corrupted." That actually applied equally to Pierre, whose early death has caused him to be overlooked. In Stockholm, when the Curies were first honored, the president of the Swedish Academy of Sciences had quoted from the book of Genesis to describe them: "It is not good that the man should be alone; I will make him an help meet for him." Marie, an agnostic, may have winced. But she could have had no grievance with his other quotation: "Union brings strength."

Justice can be slow. It took until 1995 for Marie Curie's ashes to be enshrined—next to her husband—in the Panthéon. Surrounded by memorials to great French men, she is the first woman to be honored there for her own achievements.

CHAPTER 8

Flight School:
Before Your Next Collaboration

"Wherever you go, there you are." So said Thomas à Kempis, a fifteenth-century monk devoted to lofty ideals. But he wasn't blind to the human reality—no matter how hard we try to be better, he knew that we are flawed creatures who drag our imperfections around with us.

Yes, we can work on our shortcomings. But there is only so much we can do on our own. By standing in our way and confronting us, talking with us as friends, or by collaborating with us, other people can help us grind our flaws to more manageable size.

For example: my lifelong collaboration with Frank Sinatra.

When I was very young, my mother played piano for me. Chopin, of course. Bach, always. But also the Great American Songbook and the show tunes and Tin Pan Alley hits that were standard fare in millions of households.

That was how I first encountered Sinatra, her favorite interpreter of this music. "He's the best there ever was," she said. (In distant second place? Tony Bennett.)

Over three decades, I did three dances using Sinatra's music.

My first was for a Baryshnikov piece that had Misha, in his prime, not leaving the ground. (That was one unhappy audience!) Next came *Nine Sinatra Songs,* a thirty-minute suite of duets for seven couples that is still in the repertoire of a number of dance companies around the world. And then *Sinatra Suite,* a series of dances for Baryshnikov and a partner that cast Misha in a cool, antiheroic role: the loner of "One for My Baby (and One More for the Road)."

Along the way, I stood onstage with Sinatra once in New York and once at the White House. I had one dinner with him. And, in his sweetest self-deprecating way, he paid me one over-the-top compliment: "You give me class."

My mother was thus under the impression that Frank and I were close personal friends.

Not so.

In the last few years, I've had one collaboration after another. I've traveled great distances to give lectures and explore opportunities. It's been intense and exhausting—which is, I gather, how life has lately been for a great many of us.

The greatest drain for me was *The Times They Are A-Changin'*, my collaboration with the music of Bob Dylan. Like *Movin' Out,* the dance musical I did with Billy Joel, the Dylan evening enjoyed a lot of success. Unlike *Movin' Out,* it generated a lot of controversy. And, from a commercial standpoint, it closed distressingly early.

What went wrong?

On one level, the problem wasn't me, it was Dylan's quite possessive fan base. His acolytes don't just adore him, they feel they own him. So while my interpretation of Dylan's songs was legitimate, it wasn't wise. Dylan didn't mind a new way of looking at his work. His fans did.

Looking back, I realized that I had failed to employ a cardinal tenet of this book: Tell your audience what to expect. I did not prepare them for the fact that my Dylan might not be theirs.

And on a deeper level, I had made another very basic mistake.

When I first started working with Dylan's music, I had an idea that really appealed to me—to use only Dylan's love songs. Those songs aren't what most of us think of when we list our favorite Dylan music, and Dylan's greatest hits were very important to the producers. We're used to hearing him angry and accusing, exhorting us to protest, scorning a friend who has betrayed him. But the fact is, he's also written a sheaf of gorgeous love songs and it was the sentiment in these that made me want to dance. To have used them and dramatized the relationships they suggest might have produced a show I could feel more intensely. But I had walked away from my original instinct—thus violating another of my cardinal rules—and instead, created an evening rich in pageantry and metaphor, a kind of Fellini circus.

What do you do when the world doesn't validate your vision?

I go through the stages of healing and rebirth.

Seven is a magic number for authors of self-help books—all change, it seems, is divisible by seven. I, however, count only five stages. As follows:

Start by mourning. My ideal choice would be a fortnight in the wilderness, stomping around in nature, seeing no one, until the mental and spiritual dust can settle and I'm ready to function again. Failing that, I go into my studio—a large open space in my apartment that anyone else would call a living room—and dance.

Dance what? This time, with a partner from the Dylan show, to the music of Bob Dylan. That is, to the music I would have used had I not veered off my original path—to the love songs.

I'm usually quick to cut my losses, assess my gains, and look for the next good idea. But with Dylan's material, I felt there was more I could do with the opportunities for dance that his songs presented. And I needed to know if my original instinct was the better idea. At the same time, I needed to purge any feeling of regret. So I began a round of dance as therapy, dance as a purge of demons, until my exploration and mourning were completed.

Then, in the spring of 2007, with Dylan's love songs still on the brain, three women from the *Movin' Out* cast came for tea.

"We want to dance," they announced.

"I have no jobs for you," I said.

They didn't care. They just wanted to dance: with me, with one another. Well, okay: I set them dancing.

Stage two. We're still here, a little engaged, now looking up, a little optimistic. Feeling the physical energy return. Opening eyes wide, blinkers off, newly able to see what can be learned from the last experience. Confident? Celebrate.

And look who I was celebrating with! A version of my original company of women, dancing just for the love of it. This began to call for different music. Frank Sinatra, another singer who knew a great deal about the permutations of love, came to mind.

I have so much history with his music that Sinatra feels like a return to a collaboration with an institution. That raises some strange feelings: Am I going home again? Ah, but you can't. Home's not there anymore. Even the feeling of home is an elusive, moving target.

Between the preparation and premieres of my ballets for Miami, ABT, and Seattle, we seemed to be developing material in my living room for a workshop. Eventually it became *Come Fly with Me*—an entire evening of dance set to Sinatra.

Stage three. A new idea is in play. Time to ask the pesky stage three questions: What do I need to get this done? Do I have the right tools here—a cadre of dancers who can take this project from studio to stage? I don't have to think hard about this—some of these dancers have been with me since the late 1980s. They're battle-tough. They're keepers. But what about a musical director? A designer? Business partners?

Stage four. Me. Yes, me.

Before you begin any collaboration, you must ask: Am I up to this? Do I have the physical stamina, the core strength? This is often the hardest question to answer, given our capacity for self-deception. Of course I can do this! Why would anyone think otherwise? Got to be objective here—if the leader falters, the enterprise fails.

I started working with Sean Kelleher at Edge Gym in 1985. Back then, I was a five-day-a-week gym rat. Forty minutes on an elliptical cross-trainer. Then fifteen shoulder sets, twelve abdominal sets, three leg sets, with no rest in between, all done in thirty-five minutes. I might be tiny, but I was committed—my dead lift record is 225 pounds.

But for about a year and a half, I'd fallen off the wagon. I know what changed: I'm feeling older. Disappointed, frustrated. Angry that I can't lift what once I could. Bone spur in the ankle, torn rotator cuff, bad thumb, osteoporotic back. Friends died; I've been depressed. Whatever.

The gym? No longer worth the investment.

Now I needed to come back.

Sean showed me how the personal best is still the challenge. It's not about conflict, win or lose. It's about resistance. The harder you push back, the stronger you get.

So I start going to the gym regularly but less fanatically. And not just for the physical training. I know that if I just get in the cab and go over to Edge Gym, I'll have a chance to clear my head.

As I work out, I note another change. I began my last book, *The Creative Habit,* with a description of getting into a cab at six A.M. and muttering the address of my gym. Since then, I have participated in six collaborations. And while it's a small and seemingly unconnected thing, I no longer begin my day huddled in a corner of the cab, absorbed in my thoughts and prepared to be aggravated when the driver chooses to go the long way.

Now I say "Good morning" as I close the cab door, ask the driver to make a U-turn—it's illegal, he may well decide not to do it—and suggest a route. We begin a conversation. What's the difference? My approach has changed. Because of my experiences, I'm willing to engage with the world.

Stage five. One last confrontation with myself, this one internal. My motives— what are they? Why take a fourth pass at Sinatra? Is this fresh for me? Am I eager to attack this material? Or am I losing my edge, settling, fooling myself with a rehash of old themes? Because if that's my reality, am I not asking for another disappointment? How am I operating here—out of strength or weakness?

In 1984, I trained with Teddy Atlas, a boxing legend who had, not long before, been a godsend to a lost twelve-year-old boy named Mike Tyson. I was then forty-three and about to perform in public for the first time in a few years, and I wanted to show that I hadn't lost anything. Teddy was clear that he'd give me more than a good workout: "I'm also going to teach you how to go into dark places and not get broken down." That is, he was going to train me inside and out, body and soul. He knew: Even the best fighter gets hit. Dealing with the fear and denial around that reality is crucial.

Teddy is afraid of nothing and nobody, and he'll get in your face whenever it's needed. He once had a fighter named Michael Moorer, a heavyweight contender who was such a bundle of issues that Teddy was not only his trainer but his confessor and therapist.

Teddy saw that Moorer was afraid. If he didn't lose the fear, he'd fight well—but not well enough to win. He'd tail off on his training, drink, skip his running; Moorer was always looking for an excuse. So Teddy systematically cut off his routes of escape.

In a championship bout with Evander Holyfield, Moorer kept missing opportunities to put Holyfield away; he was destined to lose on points. So at the end of the eighth round, Teddy climbed into the ring and sat on Moorer's stool. "If you don't want to fight the guy, I will!" he yelled.

Moorer didn't know what to do.

"I'm not getting up until you tell me you want to win the title," Teddy said. "Do you want to win the title?"

"Yes."

"Then you gotta show it."

And Moorer did. Barely. But enough to become the champion.

When Teddy was finished with me, I was ready to take on the world—my share of it anyway. I thought about his training a lot as I contemplated a Sinatra evening. And it became clear: I was different. There was something for me to explore here. There were new reasons for me to set one song after another. My enthusiasm was honest. And I was excited to explore it.

Our emotions are never far from the surface. They're bubbling away in offices, schools, and factories, wherever people work together. And in a dance company, they surface daily.

You find emotion in the dancers' completely unreasonable commitment to their art. You find it in the pain the dancers endure on a daily basis, the injuries they don't want the choreographer to notice. You find it in the way the dancers' energy changes when the music starts.

Love stories are a way of harnessing, dramatizing, exploding those emotions. The method is ancient: conflicts. Think of "As Time Goes By"—"a fight for love and glory." Can we avoid that fight? Only if we avoid relationships entirely. That's not a popular choice. It's downright impossible in my field if you think, as I do, that the essence of dance is relationships—sometimes partners, sometimes groups.

Couples are never generic. Just ask the participants—they all consider themselves unique. So in the new Sinatra pieces, I follow four couples during a single night in a club. I show you who comes in with whom, who leaves with whom, and what happens in between. Each character is dramatically different, but they share one belief: Other people, for all the heartache they cause us, still represent the best opportunity we have to make sense of our lives.

That is the subtext of many Sinatra songs—maybe, when you've lived long enough and piled up some emotional mileage, it's the subtext of a lot of things. It's not a new idea for me. But this time, I stumbled into a fresh perspective on the importance of relationships.

My friend Richard Avedon was a constant reader, and he often talked about his love of Marcel Proust's *In Search of Lost Time*. After Dick died, I began to read it. And the book revealed something important.

In the final volume of Proust's novel, the narrator goes to visit friends in their country house. As he enters their courtyard, he trips on some uneven paving stones. With that, "all my discouragement vanished . . . all anxiety about the future, all intellectual doubts had disappeared." He escapes the present and sees "the essence of things."

That phrase had stopped me cold. As I was building the Sinatra evening, something felt different. The words and music hadn't changed. But I had—and now, I suddenly realized, so, for me, had the essence of the songs.

When I used his music in the 1970s, I adopted the then popular view of Sinatra as a man's man: the tough talker with a bunch of male buddies, the inconstant lover who molded women to fit his needs. Male-dependent women still exist, but there are fewer of them now. More commonly, we picture a good romantic relationship as an equal partnership, with both sides struggling to avoid power trips—we picture romance as a collaboration. And so, in my latest Sinatra, women drive the plot and initiate the action as often as the men do.

As I was casting *Come Fly with Me,* I'd find myself thinking of all the men and women who had danced Sinatra for me in the past. That wasn't nostalgia. And it wasn't the notion that "everything used to be better." It was something else, something more active: a craving for dancers who could capture the essence of Sinatra.

We're not like Proust, harvesting our perceptions in the darkness of a cork-lined bedroom. For us, getting to essence is a real-world activity, played out in the open through the help—and opposition—of other people. That is, we get to essence through collaboration.

Collaboration is connection, and, suddenly, I saw how my connections to Sinatra were linked. Like this: So much of the romantic plotting of *Come Fly with Me* stems from the lessons I learned from the Dylan show. Which came out of the lessons I learned from Billy Joel's music. Which made sense to me because I had worked with Milos Forman on similar themes. And so on, back, back, back, all the way to Mom at the spinet. Can't go home again? In a way, we never leave; as Thomas à Kempis might note, we drag it around with us.

So it's the buzzword of the new millennium. But is collaboration a tool we'll continue to use?

We are a culture that consumes and discards almost in one motion. Just think of the bright ideas for more efficient and humane ways of working that have come and gone in the last few decades. Management by Objectives, Total Quality Management, Matrix Management, Team-based Management, Process Reengineering—the way they zoomed in, dominated the conversation, and disappeared, you would think these theories were fads for preteens.

Because of our insatiable appetite for novelty, I wonder if the idea of collaboration will experience a brief and superficial vogue, followed by a vivid flameout. Later, when someone suggests that we work collaboratively, we'll know exactly what to say: "That was tried, remember? The religious communities of the 1800s? The communes of the 1960s? And in so many ways around 2010? It never really worked."

Those who have committed to collaboration know better. It does work. It always did. It always will.

The only question is whether we're up to it—whether we're willing to work at it.

Reality's tutorials can be harsh. You can run your life "my way," struggling alone, or "our way," struggling to make a group effort work. Sometimes you'll succeed. Even if you do, you'll fail in the judgment of many. But beyond the scoring of your collaboration lies the real gain—the chance to interface with others and to develop a whole new tool kit of values.

Our lives are performances—each of us starring in a play we come to know as our own. Essence isn't just who you are. It's who you are with other people.

In the end, all collaborations are love stories.

- A powerful purpose makes daily annoyances smaller.
- Mutual respect makes blunt disagreement bearable.
- In time, members of a collaboration share the same emotional limits.
- Long-term collaborators know when it's "quittin' time."

Two violins, viola, cello—four sides, all equal. Does a string quartet require a leader? Its members hope not; in a creative relationship that's often compared to a marriage, the appearance of a leader is a bad sign. The creative target is harmony, not showmanship. A quartet is all about balance.

THE GUARNERI QUARTET

To play in harmony in support of a group. To control ego. And then to travel together—to live together, far from family, in anonymous hotels—week after week. The challenges are daunting.

Those are just the intimate hurdles. Until recently, quartets also lacked a business model. A conductor might be unnecessary; he was also unaffordable. Concert promoters? Uninterested. Managerial support? Few rushed in. That left the dull nitty-gritty of a show business enterprise—travel and bookings—to the musicians themselves.

And for what? Until the middle of the twentieth century, the string quartet was not considered a serious professional entity. Received wisdom had it that gifted musicians gravitated to orchestras or solo careers—they played concertos. Chamber music was for the second tier. Or, perhaps, a private amusement, performed on the side of a real career, in a drawing room.

In 1964, the prospect of an intimate creative relationship and an unfriendly business environment did not faze the members of the Guarneri

Quartet. Arnold Steinhardt, John Dalley, Michael Tree, and David Soyer (who retired in 2001 and was replaced by Peter Wiley) "just happened" to get together. And then they "just happened" to stay together until 2009, creating indelible performances and expanding the audience for chamber music until there are now a half dozen well-known quartets playing a concert somewhere tonight.

Forty-five years! In an era when half of all marriages break up, how did these four men keep theirs fresh?

Michael Tree: "We all have to have respect—mutual respect for each other. And we have to have a certain sameness, I think, of tastes . . . I think we all basically agreed on just about everything, except when it came down to the nitty-gritty of rehearsing. And that's when that question of mutual respect comes into play and it becomes very important."

Arnold Steinhardt: "We are like four brothers in a family, and we are not shy about saying 'That was too loud!' or 'We've got to fix that intonation there' or 'Why such a quick tempo? Mozart didn't write a quick tempo!' So we're aboveboard about all these things, really like people in a family who can dismiss the polite stuff, you know?"

Honesty and bluntness, but not to the point of pain. Mutual respect, but not to the point of formality and stiffness. Shared values, so the group's mission can carry it over the inevitable bumps. And, of course, actual achievement, so the group is supported by an appreciative community.

How does such a collaboration end? Without friction. The idea of quitting came up one night, and, if the members of the quartet are to be believed, there was consensus in five minutes. And why not? After forty-five years, they knew one another's minds, hearts, and souls; they had achieved the collaborative ideal.

Acknowledgments

Jesse Kornbluth, my very fine writing friend and a man of his word.

David Rosenthal, Ruth Fecych, and Julian Peploe, my teammates at Simon & Schuster. Collaborators even better the second time around.

Andrew Wylie, my agent. May we prosper together.

My validation community: Richard Burke, Gene Feldman, Robert Gottlieb, Ellen Jacobs, Bredo Johnsen, Ginger Montel, Norma Stevens, Patsy Tarr.

Four generations of dancers who help me extend the past into the present.